SPEC OPS ™

OFFICIAL STRATEGIES & SECRETS ™

Chris Jensen
Doug Radcliffe

SYBEX®

San Francisco • Paris • Düsseldorf • Soest

Associate Publisher: Roger Stewart
Contracts and Licensing Manager: Kristine Plachy
Acquisitions and Publications Manager: Dan Brodnitz
Managing Editor Game Books: Tory McLearn
Editor: Bonnie Britt
Project Manager: Lisa Auer
Proofreader: Lisa Auer
Book Design: Franz Baumhackl
Book Production: Van Winkle Design Group
Cover Designer: Calyx Designs

Library of Congress Card Number: 2457-98-88837
ISBN: 0-7821-2457-7
Manufactured in the United States of America

10 9 8 7 6 5 4 3 2

ACKNOWLEDGMENTS

The authors would like to thank the following people for their generous support toward the creation of this book: Dan Brodnitz (a high-level character), Mark Long for getting us the needed materials, Bill Wright for coming through in the clutch, Lisa Auer, Franz Baumhackl, Bonnie Britt, Tory McLearn, and Diana Van Winkle.

TABLE OF CONTENTS

INTRODUCTION   iX

PART I BASIC TRAINING   1

CHAPTER 1
BRIEF HISTORY OF THE U.S. ARMY RANGERS   3

HUMBLE BEGINNINGS   5

THE CIVIL WAR   5

THE SECOND WORLD WAR   6

VIETNAM   7

THE IRANIAN CRISIS   8

SOMALIA   10

CHAPTER 2
BOOT CAMP—WELCOME TO BASIC TRAINING   13

CONFIGURING COMBAT CONTROL   15

DIFFICULTY SETTINGS   19

SPEC OPS INTERFACE   20

CAMERA VIEWS   24

CHAPTER 3
WEAPONS AND EQUIPMENT 29

ASSAULT RIFLES 31

EXPLOSIVES 33

MACHINE GUNS 36

SCOPES 38

SHOTGUN 40

SNIPER RIFLES 40

MISCELLANEOUS EQUIPMENT 42

PART II COMBAT TACTICS 43

CHAPTER 4
SINGLE-PLAYER TACTICS 45

THE SEVEN DEADLY SKILLS 47

ORDERING YOUR PARTNER 47

POSTURES 51

SNIPING 54

SITUATIONAL AWARENESS 57

OUTFITTING 58

MONITORING THE GPS 59

CHANGING RANGERS 60

CHAPTER 5
DEATHMATCH STRATEGY — 61

GENERAL DEATHMATCH STRATEGIES — 63

DEATHMATCH MAP STRATEGIES — 68

CHAPTER 6
CO-OP AND TEAM TACTICS — 79

CO-OP AND TEAM PLAY BRIEFING — 81

COMMUNICATION — 81

FORMATIONS — 83

BATTLE PLAN — 85

PART III MISSION WALKTHROUGHS — 89

CHAPTER 7
RUSSIA—THE VORONYE FOREST — 91

MISSION 1—PHASE 1 — 93

MISSION 1—PHASE 2 — 96

MISSION 1—PHASE 3 — 99

CHAPTER 8
NORTH KOREA—KAPSAN MISSILE BASE — 103

MISSION 2—PHASE 1 — 105

MISSION 2—PHASE 2 — 108

MISSION 2—PHASE 3 — 110

MISSION 2—PHASE 4 — 113

CHAPTER 9
COLOMBIA—THE MAGDALENA RIVER — 117

MISSION 3–PHASE 1 — 119

MISSION 3–PHASE 2 — 122

MISSION 3–PHASE 3 — 124

CHAPTER 10
HONDURAS—SIERRA DE SOCONUSCO — 129

MISSION 4–PHASE 1 — 131

MISSION 4–PHASE 2 — 133

MISSION 4–PHASE 3 — 136

CHAPTER 11
AFGHANISTAN—THE CITY OF KABUL — 141

MISSION 5–PHASE 1 — 143

MISSION 5–PHASE 2 — 146

MISSION 5–PHASE 3 — 149

CHAPTER 12
PALE, BOSNIA—1998 — 153

MISSION 6–PHASE 1 — 155

MISSION 6–PHASE 2 — 159

MISSION 6–PHASE 3 — 162

CHAPTER 13
THON AN THAI, VIETNAM—1969   167

MISSION 7—PHASE 1   169

MISSION 7—PHASE 2   172

MISSION 7—PHASE 3   176

CHAPTER 14
RAYAT, IRAQ—1996   179

MISSION 8—PHASE 1   181

MISSION 8—PHASE 2   184

MISSION 8—PHASE 3   187

APPENDIX A
SPEC OPS SCORING SYSTEM   191

AWARD SCREEN   193

MEDALS   194

APPENDIX B
INTERNET RESOURCES   197

WEB SITES   199

MODIFICATIONS   204

PATCHES   205

GLOSSARY   207

INTRODUCTION

Spec Ops is unlike anything you've played before because it is the first realistic Army Ranger simulation. Lead designer and Zombie cofounder Mark Long, an ex-U.S. Army Ranger, designed and developed *Spec Ops* with the assistance of the 2/75th Ranger Battalion.

To reflect the look of real soldiers in action, Long applied motion-capture technology for Ranger animation, in which character movement is controlled by an actor hooked up to a set of sensors. Zombie's motion-capture actor is a former Green Beret. The texture maps that make up the Ranger player models were borrowed from real photos. All of the game's sound effects, such as gunfire and grenade explosions, came from live sources. Combined, these elements have created the most realistic simulation of Ranger combat and tactics yet devised.

Nearly every first-person shooter on the market stakes a claim to fast-paced action that requires little in the way of strategy or planning. This isn't to say that *Spec Ops* doesn't have its fair share of intense violence, something you'll see first hand when you land in the jungles of Vietnam.

Where *Spec Ops* differs is in its use of tactics and cunning. Instead of running around a dank dungeon, charging into rooms and shooting at anything that moves, the *Spec Ops* environment demands patience, planning, and nerves of steel.

Once you've outfitted your Rangers and studied the mission briefing, you're off to any number of foreign countries in a variety of decades. One mission will have you securing a landing zone in 1995 Russian Voronye, while another will transport you back to 1965 Vietnam in a desperate search-and-rescue mission for a downed B-52 pilot. All the while, you will be up against impossible odds, facing a determined enemy that may have a sniper's site aimed right between your eyes. Expect the enemy to lob grenades, plant booby traps, set up ambushes, and call for reinforcements. They'll be hidden in foxholes, rooted in towers, hiding behind trucks, and crawling along the jungle floor. They'll give you everything they have, and will try every possible way to stop your mission. You'd better be ready for them.

In order to succeed in *Spec Ops,* you'll need to be skilled in a variety of areas. Most games expect you to shoot straight, but *Spec Ops* will test your ability to plan ahead, command a small unit, outfit your men with the proper tools, scout unknown terrain, and plant explosives. That's where this book will help. Created with the full cooperation of Zombie VR Studios, *Spec Ops Official Strategies & Secrets* will serve as your military bible, covering everything you need to know to lead your squad to victory.

WHAT'S IN THIS BOOK

Whether you're a green recruit straight off the bus from Anywhere, USA, or a seasoned veteran in need of a refresher course, *Spec Ops Official Strategies & Secrets* will prove a valuable reference. Appendix A describes the scoring system and displays medals and awards you can win for skill and bravery. Appendix B covers many Internet resources devoted to the game *Spec Ops*. The glossary lists common (and not so common) military terms.

The book is divided into three parts:

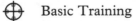 Basic Training

⊕ Combat Tactics

⊕ Mission Walkthroughs

WHICH VERSION OF SPEC OPS DOES THIS BOOK COVER?

Spec Ops: Rangers Lead the Way was released in the first half of 1998. In the fall of '98, Zombie and Ripcord followed with an add-on pack called *Spec Ops: Ranger Team Bravo* as well as a combination set featuring the original game *and* the add-on pack. This book covers all three versions of the game with two caveats:

1. Since the original release, Zombie and Ripcord have posted a few patches to the game that add gameplay features, including the ability to outfit your squad prior to a mission. Our mission walkthroughs assume you've got the new features. If you've installed Ranger Team Bravo or the combination set, you're ready to go. If you bought the original game and haven't picked up the add-on pack, be sure to take advantage of these free online patches and upgrade your *Spec Ops* to the latest version. See Appendix B for details on where to find *Spec Ops* patches on the Web.

2. Ranger Team Bravo gives the player all of the enhancements of the patch, as well as exclusive features like three new campaign settings and even Internet multiplayer.

PART 1: BASIC TRAINING

This is where it all begins—the perfect start for the new player who wants to get up to speed before taking it to the enemy. Your experience begins with a brief history of the U.S. Army Rangers, their role, where they've been, what they've done, and most importantly, how critical they've been in keeping peace across the world. Chapter 2 covers the configuration of your controls, how to issue in-game commands, and how to coordinate the many different camera views within the game. Chapter 3 addresses available weaponry and equipment for missions, as well as tactics for each firearm.

PART 2: COMBAT TACTICS

The enemy will show no mercy on the battlefield. He'll take advantage of every mistake. To succeed, you'd better be at your peak. Combat tactics in Chapter 4 will aid your quest for domination. You'll pick up solid tips applicable to any mission and get expert advice on commanding your squad and moving across the battlefield like a seasoned veteran. Chapter 5 is the resource for taking on opponents in Internet play. It offers deathmatch tips and strategies for each of the multiplayer maps within the game. Chapter 6 takes multiplayer one step further with tips and strategies for team and co-op play.

PART 3: MISSION WALKTHROUGHS

This is where you'll put everything you've learned into action. Each of the missions and phases that comprise the *Spec Ops* experience are there, along with helpful hints and strategies to get out of any situation. We'll recommend what equipment to take on each mission and what items to leave behind.

NOTE It's possible to outfit your Rangers differently from what we recommended in the Squad Selection sections and still be successful, so feel free to experiment if you'd like.

APPENDIXES AND GLOSSARY

The back of the book offers useful references. It includes a handy military glossary, information on the medals you'll be awarded throughout your *Spec Ops* tour of duty, Internet resources, fan sites, and actual U.S. Army Ranger sites. You'll learn how to modify your *Spec Ops* experience by downloading third-party programs.

Now let's get ready for combat!

PART I

Basic Training

Welcome to boot camp, soldier. Before you receive your mission orders and venture off into foreign lands, take this opportunity to get familiar with *Spec Ops*. All recruits are asked to study the history of the U.S. Army Rangers to gain a better understanding of their role within the military. Next you'll begin your training by getting a handle on the *Spec Ops* interface, creating a custom control configuration, and learning how best to handle the many camera angles available. Finally, we'll take you into the *Spec Ops* warehouse and explain the weapons and equipment you can access, as well as items found on the enemy. Let's get moving!

CHAPTER 1

Brief History of the U.S. Army Rangers

Before you complete basic training and head out into your first tour of duty, study the history of the most challenging branch of the United States military. U.S. Army Rangers are unlike any other service and have taken part in many conflicts since the birth of the United States. Their numbers are few, their skills immeasurable, and you're about to join their ranks.

"Rangers Lead the Way!" is the motto of United States Army Rangers, a unique breed of soldiers who trace their roots from the 17th century in colonial America until today. From their humble beginnings, Rangers have been warriors who combine guts with a talent for warfare. Here's a quick look at some notable moments in the history of the U.S. Rangers.

HUMBLE BEGINNINGS

The Rangers go as far back as frontiersmen in the New World. Early settlers encountered stiff resistance from native tribes who engaged in a style of combat that was alien to the settlers. Using long-range scouting, concealment, and raids, Native Americans inflicted heavy casualties on the colonists. The settlers responded by adapting. They applied this new style of warfare against some tribes native to the northeast. Groups of colonists left the settlements and searched for raiding parties. When they returned, the colonists reported they had "ranged" or patrolled a certain distance from their homes. That led to naming these scouts Rangers. The first official Ranger unit was activated in 1670 to fight a Native American tribe under the leadership of Metocomet. The Rangers, led by Captain Benjamin Church, stopped the attacks on colonists and ended King Philip's War in 1676.

THE CIVIL WAR

When war broke out between the Union and secessionist states, the Confederacy employed Ranger tactics with great success. Colonel John S. Mosby organized his Rangers in Virginia. From a three-man scout unit in 1862, Mosby's force grew to an operation of eight companies of Rangers by 1865. Mosby was heavily influenced by Francis Marion, a widely respected warrior during the Revolutionary War who developed battle tactics that found their way into the Ranger modus operandi. Mosby adopted a style of strategic operations that confused Union officers and left them wondering where he would strike next. The Rangers fed off this confusion, forcing exhausted Federal units to pull needed troops from the front lines to reinforce several positions. Mosby selected weak targets to deal crushing blows.

Mosby's Rangers were excellent riflemen and horsemen who understood the Virginia terrain. They were so confident of their mastery of the terrain that they carried out night operations, a first for that time.

The Union's only notable employment of Rangers was the capture of Confederate General James Longstreet's ammunition train.

When the Civil War ended, Army Ranger units disappeared for more than 70 years.

THE SECOND WORLD WAR

On June 19, 1942, at Carrickfergus, Northern Ireland, 2,000 hand-picked volunteers led by U.S. Army Major William O. Darby endured rigorous training by British commandos. Many dropped out of training and, by the end, only 500 were left. They became the 1st Ranger Battalion. Fifty of these Rangers, along with Canadian and British regiments, took part in the August 19, 1942, raid on Dieppe on France's northeast coast. This commando attack to test the strength of German defenses was a disaster, but later excursions were effective.

In November 1942, the Marines and the 1st Ranger Battalion went ashore at Arzeu, Algeria, and moved overland to the port of Oran, where they occupied the strategic Spanish fortress at the northern tip of the harbor.

They carried out critical night operations in Tunisia and participated in the Battle of El Guettar. On March 31, 1943, the 1st Ranger Battalion led the drive by General George S. Patton Jr. to capture the heights of El Guettar with a 12-mile night march across mountainous terrain. The strategy surprised enemy positions from the rear. By dawn, the Rangers swooped down on stunned Italian fascists and cleared the El Guettar Pass with the capture of 200 prisoners. For this action, the 1st Ranger Battalion won its first Presidential Citation—the equivalent of awarding each man the Distinguished Service Cross.

Major Darby created two more battalions, the 3rd and 4th, toward the end of the campaign in Tunisia. These battalions, along with the 1st, were called "Darby's Rangers" or the Ranger Force. They led the invasion of Sicily at Gela and Licata and played a role in the taking of Messina. At Salerno they fought off eight German counterattacks for 18 days to hold the Chunzi Pass. The Rangers endured the fierce winter and mountain combat in clearing the entrance to the narrow pass leading to Cassino. At Anzio, they defeated German beach defenses and secured the town.

During the assault on Omaha Beach, Brigadier General Norman D. Cota, assistant division commander of the 29th Infantry Division, realized that the invasion force had to push past the beach or suffer severe losses. He chose the Rangers of the 5th Battalion led by Lieutenant Colonel Max Schneider to make way through the overwhelming fire with the command "Rangers, lead the way off this beach!" General Cota's order became the familiar motto, "Rangers lead the way."

VIETNAM

In Vietnam the LRRPs (Long Range Reconnaissance Patrols) continued the Ranger lineage. Thirteen companies were assigned to brigades, divisions, and field units to act as eyes and ears inside land claimed by the Viet Cong and North Vietnamese Army. They worked in small groups and relied on stealth to evade enemy observation. LRRP teams also attacked the Viet Cong using surprise raids and ambushes. The LRRPs were redesignated the 75th Infantry Regiment (Ranger) on June 1, 1969. The LRRP/ Rangers were disbanded at the end of the Vietnam War.

THE IRANIAN CRISIS

The frustrating pattern of activating and then deactivating Ranger units after a crisis finally ended in 1973. Army Chief of Staff General Creighton W. Abrams called for the creation of a permanent Ranger presence in the Army. The 1st Ranger Battalion was activated on February 8, 1974, at Fort Stewart, Georgia. The 2nd Ranger Battalion was formed on October 1, 1974. The 1st Battalion established headquarters at Hunter Army Airfield, Georgia, while the 2nd Battalion dug in at Fort Lewis, Washington.

    The ill-fated attempt in 1980 to rescue American Embassy personnel held hostage by students in Teheran, Iran, was code-named Desert One. It was primarily a Special Forces Operation. It is not generally known that Rangers took part. While 1st Special Forces Operational Detachment Delta performed the actual rescue, Company C, 1st Battalion, provided security for men and equipment.

The rescue force gathered in Egypt on April 21, 1980. Three days later, several C-141s carried 120 men to Masirah Island, off the coast of Oman, where they transferred to three MC-130s accompanied by three fuel-bearing EC-130s. They landed 200 miles southeast of Teheran at 2200 hours and awaited eight RH-53D Sea Stallion helicopters from the aircraft carrier *Nimitz*. A 12-man road watch team, composed of Rangers, secured the site while the helicopters refueled.

The task of C 1/75 was to secure a landing area for the transports. The Rangers were to fly from Egypt to Manazariyeh, Iran, and secure the airfield. They were to land, if possible, or jump if there was resistance. Once the airfield was secure, the Rangers were to hold it while C-141s arrived to airlift the hostages and their rescuers back to Egypt. The Rangers were then to remove all signs of their presence, render the field useless, and be airlifted out.

Taking and securing a hostile airfield within enemy territory was one of the primary components of the Ranger mission. They were ready to hold the field for as long as necessary if there were not enough transports to take everyone out in one trip.

Desert One was aborted at the first stage when one of the helicopters developed a hydraulics problem. Later two helicopters crashed into each other on landing and killed the crew. It had been determined that at least six helicopters were necessary for the mission to succeed. The rescue attempt was canceled automatically when there were fewer than six. The C 1/75 never left Egypt. The Rangers returned with the Delta special operations group.

SOMALIA

The next deployment of the Rangers occurred in Somalia in 1993. Battalion 3/75 was deployed for less than two months—August 26, 1993, to October 21, 1993— to assist United Nations forces to bring order to a chaotic and starving nation. The Rangers took part in seven missions in an attempt to capture fugitive strongman General Mohammed Farah Aidid and his top lieutenants. The goal was to end Aidid's guerrilla war against UN efforts to feed the Somali people.

General Aidid's militia shot down a U.S. helicopter on September 25, 1993, killing three infantrymen. Rangers moved in after the Black Hawk was downed. Under fire from machine guns and hand and rocket propelled grenades, the Rangers grouped together and established a perimeter inside buildings to help their wounded and wait for relief. The relief column, composed of cooks and other Rangers, took heavy fire en route to their fellow Rangers.

The Rangers lost six men and had many wounded. The Somali warlord fared far worse—the Rangers and UN forces delivered lethal firepower and killed approximately 300 of his forces, and many more were wounded.

RANGER CREED

Recognizing that I volunteered as a Ranger, fully knowing the hazards of my chosen profession, I will always endeavor to uphold the prestige, honor, and high esprit de corps of the Rangers.

Acknowledging the fact that a Ranger is a more elite soldier who arrives at the cutting edge of battle by land, sea, or air, I accept the fact that as a Ranger my country expects me to move further, faster, and fight harder than any other soldier.

Never shall I fail my comrades. I will always keep myself mentally alert, physically strong, and morally straight and I will shoulder more than my share of the task whatever it may be, one hundred percent and then some.

Gallantly will I show the world that I am a specially selected and well trained soldier. My courtesy to superior officers, neatness of dress, and care of equipment shall set the example for others to follow.

Energetically will I meet the enemies of my country. I shall defeat them on the field of battle for I am better trained and will fight with all my might. Surrender is not a Ranger word. I will never leave a fallen comrade to fall into the hands of the enemy and under no circumstances will I ever embarrass my country. Readily will I display the intestinal fortitude required to fight on to the Ranger objective and complete the mission, though I be the lone survivor.

CHAPTER 2

Boot Camp—
Welcome to
Basic Training

Before you dive into the heat of battle, take time to learn the details. Every warrior has to pass Boot Camp training before moving on to the real deal, or they'll learn the hard way.

This chapter covers everything from creating a custom control layout to properly coordinating the many camera views available from within the game. Each element is important and will further your enjoyment of the *Spec Ops* experience.

CONFIGURING COMBAT CONTROL

There are several different ways to control your Ranger in *Spec Ops* with a gamepad, mouse, keyboard, or even a combination of the three. Unlike most action/strategy games, *Spec Ops* lets the player customize the control scheme. With that in mind, don't treat these guidelines as gospel. If you're comfortable with the default control settings in *Spec Ops*, skip this section and move on. However, a few small changes to the default setup can make a big difference.

KEYBOARD CONTROL

Keyboard control is the lifeblood of *Spec Ops*, offering every game option available on one key or another. Most players will want to change the location of these keys to maximize their experience.

The default keyboard setup is cumbersome for some players. When the action in *Spec Ops* reaches a frenetic level, with screams coming from a dark grove of trees and sniper fire riddling the ground at your feet, well, this is no time to divert your eyes and fumble for a key. When a decision is needed and you have to act within a split second, you want the right key at the tip of your finger. By creating a custom keyboard layout (see Figure 2.1) that feels right, desired moves will be at your fingertips.

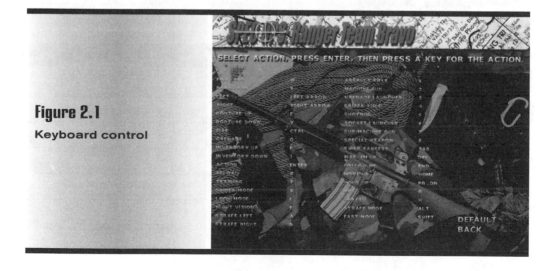

Figure 2.1
Keyboard control

MOVEMENT KEYS

Spec Ops places the movement buttons on the arrow keys at the right side of your keyboard, which is common with most first-person games. However, there is a more efficient location for these keys, a place we call WSAD.

Forward	Back	Strafe Left	Strafe Right
W	S	A	D

The primary benefit of the WSAD system is that it places the movement controls closer to the weapon selection keys, while offering plenty of other keys close by that can be used for important commands.

Viewing the keyboard, we see eight keys within a finger's reach, not including the weapon keys (1–8), that are open for whatever you wish. This is more efficient than the default layout.

MISCELLANEOUS COMMANDS

Besides movement, there are other commands you'll want to move around. What follows is a sample setup that offer the most important commands in the most convenient spots.

Action	Key
Posture Up	E
Posture Down	C
Grenade	Q
Sniper Mode	X
Night Vision	F

We've maximized the territory around the movement keys and assigned critical game functions to buttons you can reach without looking at the keyboard.

WARNING Be sure you don't accidentally allocate more than one command to the same button.

Alter this setup however you wish—with different commands in various locations—but be sure to use these keys. They'll make a difference in your mission's success.

GAMEPAD/JOYSTICK

Playing *Spec Ops* with a gamepad or joystick isn't the most convenient way to enter battle, but for those of you who are comfortable with joysticks and gamepads, we can still offer a few tips. Your success with a gamepad or joystick depends on how many buttons you have. Traditionally, most joysticks and gamepads have just a few, forcing the *Spec Ops* player to rely on the keyboard for most of the game while switching to the gamepad/joystick for firing and movement

TIP If you're going to use a joystick, be sure to use every button available for critical game commands.

You should have at least eight buttons on your joystick before you even consider using it for *Spec Ops*. This will let you allocate the most important game functions within range of your trigger finger

Button	Function
1	Fire
2	Grenade
3	Action
4	Sniper Mode
5	Posture Up
6	Posture Down
7	Inventory Up
8	Inventory Down

Your next step after setting up the joystick is to rearrange a few keyboard commands to the left side of the keyboard (if you're right-handed). This will give you an advantage and allow you to grip the joystick while pressing the needed keyboard command. See Figure 2.2 for our suggested gamepad/joystick configuration.

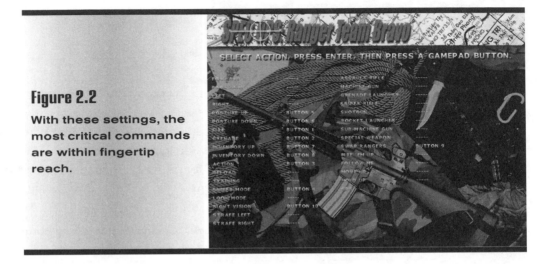

Figure 2.2

With these settings, the most critical commands are within fingertip reach.

Mouse

For the ultimate in playing *Spec Ops*, use the mouse in conjunction with the keyboard. The combination gives you complete control over speed and precision. With this setup, you can control turning ability far faster than with a gamepad/joystick and you can use the left hand to move forward, back, and strafe right or left.

If you've never used the mouse/keyboard combination for a first-person shooter, try it now. While it may not seem natural at first, a few minutes of play will lead to total control.

Most *Spec Ops* players have a two-button mouse, while a few have the added benefit of three.

Mouse Button	Command
Left	Fire
Right	Look
Center	Grenade

With a three-button mouse, we moved the grenade key to the middle button, a command initially assigned to the Q key on the keyboard. Q is now free for whatever command you wish, allowing for faster firepower with the press of a mouse button.

By placing the Look command on the right mouse button, you can scan around your soldier with a convenient mouse-click instead of fumbling around the keyboard. See Figure 2.3 for a suggested mouse control configuration.

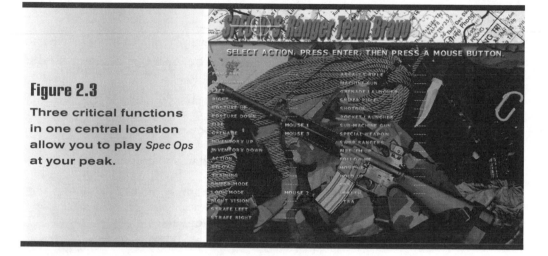

Figure 2.3

Three critical functions in one central location allow you to play *Spec Ops* at your peak.

DIFFICULTY SETTINGS

Three difficulty settings in *Spec Ops* will drastically affect the style of game you play. Choose an option based on your current ability. Additionally, difficulty settings can lend themselves to replaying the game several times, one for each level of difficulty.

The three difficulty settings are:

- Private (Easy)
- Corporal (Medium)
- Sergeant (Difficult)

If you're experienced with a wide variety of first-person shooters, consider playing at the Corporal level. If you're somewhat new to this game genre, ease yourself in by playing at the Private level. For the hardest of hardcore players, the Sergeant level will offer the most brutal experience possible.

 TIP To increase your replay value, set Random Enemies to on.

What's the difference between difficulty levels? Unlike a lot of first-person shooters that would simply throw more enemies at you, *Spec Ops* increases the difficulty in a more realistic fashion, not through sheer numbers.

Four parameters are changed by increasing the difficulty level:

⊕ Private level enemies have 100 damage points.

⊕ Corporal level enemies have 250 damage points.

⊕ Sergeant level enemies have 450 damage points.

⊕ Enemy accuracy increases 100% for each skill level.

SPEC OPS INTERFACE

By now you should have a very good control scheme in place, ready to tackle whatever the enemy tosses at you. Before rushing into battle half-cocked, learn a little more about the *Spec Ops* interface. A thorough understanding of information displayed during the game can make the difference between a successful mission and embarrassing failure.

The main game screen of *Spec Ops* can be broken down into the seven regions shown in Figure 2.4.

Figure 2.4

The *Spec Ops* Interface

HEALTH

Displays the current health of your Ranger. If the gauge is green, you're in fine condition. Once it hits yellow, you've sustained moderate damage but aren't yet in a life-threatening situation. If red is all you see, you've taken severe damage from the enemy and are close to death.

 **WARNING** If you're in critical shape, find cover as fast as possible and use your medkit to heal yourself. If you don't have a medkit handy, search your surroundings until you find one.

BODY ARMOR

If you happen to find a flak vest during a mission, the Body Armor display will come to life and show you how much damage it can take. They're beneficial for the sole reason that any enemy fire you take will be subtracted from the flak vest before it hits your personal health. A flak vest will give you a definite advantage over the enemy.

INVENTORY

This is where you'll find the bulk of your starting items, including the ever-important GPS and Starcom. You'll also find grenades, medkits, and night-vision goggles in your pack when you first start a mission.

To select a new item in your inventory, simply press either bracket key to toggle up or down until the item you want to use is highlighted. Obviously, these keys may be different if you changed the default system under Keyboard Configuration. Any additional items you get during a mission will be put into the inventory.

 NOTE The GPS and night goggles can be used at the same time.

SCOPE INVENTORY

Similar to the Inventory, this area lists any scopes you currently carry. Press the Sniper button on the keyboard (or wherever you assigned it) and a short list of items will come up. You'll almost always have access to a pair of binoculars and an ACOG, both of which are selected by pressing either bracket key. If you have a weapon that can be outfitted with a scope, you'll see 2X or 4X or sometimes both. Both scopes function like binoculars with the added benefit of an aiming indicator, allowing for very precise shooting.

WEAPON IN USE

This display indicates the weapon you've chosen, the number of rounds in the clip, and the number of clips you currently have. If you're running low on rounds, take the time to scout around for extra ammo. Often, fallen enemies will leave behind boxes of ammo that may or may not fit your particular weapon.

Keeping a close eye on how many rounds are in your current clip is important, especially for weapons with a high fire rate. Just as in real life, the weapons in *Spec Ops* must be reloaded when a clip goes dry. There is no worse time to discover an expired clip than in the middle of a firefight. When that happens, you're forced to take critical seconds away from defending yourself to reload. Usually that process ends with you lying, face first, in a pool of blood.

 TIP Always monitor the clip in your weapon to be sure you're entering combat fully loaded. Finding out the hard way that you're low on ammo does not serve the needs of the U.S. Army Rangers.

CURRENT INVENTORY ITEM

SATCOM RADIO

This handy display depicts which item in your inventory is ready for use. It also tells if you currently have a grenade or other explosive ready. To use whatever item is listed, press the Enter key.

 WARNING Make sure you know which item is ready before you enter a firefight. It's easy to err when the action kicks in, and sometimes what you thought was a grenade turns out to be a satchel charge.

MISSION TIMER

1599:33

If a mission has a time limit, a countdown clock appears in this area. Keep a close eye on it and don't dillydally. There's nothing more frustrating than wiping out the enemy and nearly succeeding in your objective, only to fail because you were 30 seconds too late.

 TIP There's plenty of time to explore after the primary objective has been accomplished. Use your time wisely.

CAMERA VIEWS

Quite a few players fail to use the various camera views in *Spec Ops* effectively. Unlike the majority of first-person shooters on the market, *Spec Ops* allows for quite a few views. Each has a particular strength. Let's take a look at each available view and see how it fits into your gameplan.

ORBITING CAMERA

The Orbiting Camera is a unique view that, when toggled on, will slowly revolve around your Ranger, affording a good view of the entire surrounding. When used in conjunction with the night-vision goggles, it can be an effective method for scouting out nearby surroundings without moving an inch.

The Orbiting Camera can be toggled off when the view reaches a point you'd like to lock on. For instance, if you have a hunch there may be some enemy activity behind you, let the Orbiting Camera view your Ranger from straight ahead, allowing you to see any enemies who may be pursuing. See Figure 2.5 for a straight-on view.

Figure 2.5

Looking at your ranger with the Orbiting Camera

OVER-THE-SHOULDER CAMERA

The Over-the-Shoulder Camera (OTS) is the default view for *Spec Ops* and most likely what you'll use for the majority of the game. This allows for a tight view of your Ranger, making it pretty simple to line up your shots and determine your heading. While the OTS Camera is fairly close to the Ranger, it maintains a decent view of the peripheral, making it a solid camera view for just about any situation (see Figure 2.6).

Figure 2.6
Over-the-Shoulder
Camera

SIDE VIEW CAMERA

The Side View Camera is an important view for quickly checking out the landscape to your right or left. The trick is to tap the Side View Camera rapidly and often, allowing for a quick glimpse of your sides while returning to a forward view. You don't want to linger on either side for too long, for every second you spend gazing in one direction is another second the enemy has to sneak up from behind or in front of you (see Figure 2.7).

Figure 2.7
Side View Camera

OVERHEAD CAMERA

The Overhead Camera displays the action, not surprisingly, from directly overhead your Ranger, pulled back far enough to offer you a wide angle of view (see Figure 2.8). This view helps when climbing a hill, navigating thick foliage, or trying to figure out the exact location of your partner. Staying in Overhead Camera view too long can expose you to enemy activity.

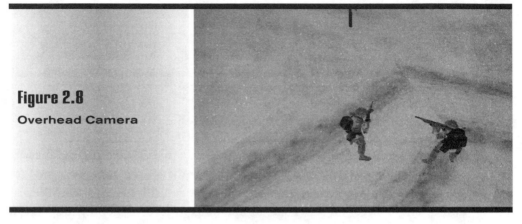

Figure 2.8
Overhead Camera

INTERIOR CAMERA

The Interior Camera is the view of choice when your Ranger is surrounded by thick foliage or investigating the interior of a structure. Because the view is virtually first person, this minimizes the possibility of your view being obstructed by a nearby object (see Figure 2.9).

Figure 2.9
Interior Camera

SNIPER CAMERA

The Sniper Camera is the most powerful view available. When it's activated, your view will change to a first-person perspective and, best of all, gain the benefit of magnification, whether you're using an ACOG, binoculars, or a scope outfitted to your weapon.

WARNING Staying in Sniper Camera view too long can be hazardous to your health. While it's an exceptional camera when moving forward, it doesn't allow for much in the way of peripheral vision, exposing your sides and rear to enemy ambush.

The ACOG is the easiest view to maintain while moving your Ranger through the level, as the view isn't magnified nearly as much as the binoculars or scopes (see Figure 2.10). This gives you the best of all worlds—a solid view of your surroundings, the advantage of increased visual range, and the ability to pick off targets that would normally remain hidden in the distance.

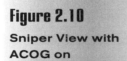

Figure 2.10

Sniper View with ACOG on

NOTE You cannot use your night-vision goggles while in Sniper Camera mode.

CHAPTER 3

Weapons and Equipment

Before you outfit your Rangers, take the time to fully understand the strengths and weaknesses of each weapon. What you bring to the heart of combat can make all the difference in the successful completion of a mission. Without a proper understanding of the *Spec Ops* arsenal, you could find yourself stuck in a rut, faced with a clear objective, but lacking the tools to complete the task.

The skilled Ranger will study the equipment and select the right tool for the job. A strategic blend of items is the only way to ensure that you and your partner are properly armed. Each weapon has unique strengths and weaknesses.

ASSAULT RIFLES

The rifle is a precise, low-rate-of-fire weapon that excels in picking off the enemy from long range. Rifles are compatible with all of the available scopes in *Spec Ops,* which permits you to take out the enemy from beyond visual range without their knowing you're there.

AK74

The AK74 is a highly effective automatic weapon designed for the antipersonnel role at a range of 1,000 meters. The system automation operates on propellant gases driven through a vent in the barrel. The 5.56-mm AK74 is an updated version of the 5.45-mm AK74 designed to comply with NATO standard cartridges. A plastic butt is furnished. The design features a basic individual infantry weapon. The complete set includes a knife and scabbard-cutter kit that can be used as a bayonet.

If you're taking hits from long range in *Spec Ops,* chances are the enemy has an AK74 trained on you. While the AK74 pumps out more bullets than the average rifle in a single burst, it takes a bit longer to shoot a second burst.

The AK74 inflicts less damage than the M4, ultimately making it less effective than its bigger brother. While you can't loadout the AK74, you'll be able to outfit it if a fallen enemy drops one. If you've already got an M4 when you come across an AK74, it never hurts to have more than one option. If nothing else, the AK74 is a little more helpful in close combat than the M4.

Weapon	Damage	Burst Count	Loadout Wgt.	Burst Delay	Clip Wgt.
AK74	75	4	N/A	1.0/sec	N/A

G11

The HK G11 is gas operated with a cyclic rate of fire of 2,000 rpm, utilizing a floating interior system where the barrel, magazine, and breech recoil within a synthetic housing. Fifty round magazines and optical sights complete the package. In 1990, extensive testing showed that of 60,000 rounds fired, estimated ammunition failure rate was about 1/485 rounds, with a minimum cook-off rate of 150 rounds at 60 rpm.

The G11 is chambered to fire a 4.73 × 33-mm caseless round, whereas the HK-ACR fires 4.92 × 34-mm caseless rounds. In Germany, the caliber of the bore diameter is measured from land to land. In the United States, caliber is measured from groove to groove. The length of the cartridge of the G11 and HK-ACR is 33-mm long. In the United States, the length of the chamber, not the cartridge case, describes the round.

The G11 is an exceptional close quarters combat weapon, especially when securing a building or attempting to take out several enemies quickly. While the damage isn't exceptional, this is made up for by the rapid fire rate.

Weapon	Damage	Burst Count	Loadout Wgt.	Burst Delay	Clip Wgt.
G11	65	4	5 kg	.4/sec	1

M203 and M16

The M203 40-mm grenade launcher is a single-shot weapon designed for use with the M16 rifle series. It fires a 40-mm grenade. The M203A1 grenade launcher is a single-shot weapon designed for use with the M16 carbine series. It also fires a 40-mm grenade.

WARNING You cannot reload the M203 from the prone position.

The M203 fires a small antipersonnel grenade that creates a significant amount of damage in a small radius. The damage rating is virtually pointless since anyone within the radius will be killed. The primary strength of the M203 is its ability to lob a grenade a considerable distance, much farther than you could throw from a standing position. While this is beneficial for clearing a long-range area, the M203 is also an excellent decoy weapon. By lobbing grenades in the opposite direction of your travel, you keep the enemy guessing where you're heading. You never know, one of those stray grenades could always hit the enemy by accident. Of course, the opposite is true as well, especially during a team or co-op game. Extreme caution should be used when toting the M203 into combat.

Weapon	Damage	Burst Count	Loadout Wgt.	Burst Delay	Clip Wgt.
M16	100	3	4 kg	.5/sec	1
M203	special	1	8 kg	.5/sec	1

M4

The M4 is a lightweight, gas-operated, air-cooled, magazine-fed, selective-rate, shoulder-fired weapon with a collapsible stock. A shortened variant of the M16A2 rifle, the M4 provides the individual soldier operating in close quarters with the capability to engage targets at extended range with accurate, lethal fire.

The strength of the M4 is its long-range accuracy and ability to accommodate any scope. Its short-range usefulness is suspect, however, and if you are rushed by enemies, the M4 is weak for dealing with the situation. Its low burst rate will find you a sitting duck when the action comes on hot and heavy unless your accuracy is pin-point perfect. With this in mind, the M4 should only be taken into combat if you're confident the bulk of enemy activity will take place at medium to long range.

Weapon	Damage	Burst Count	Loadout Wgt.	Burst Delay	Clip Wgt.
M4	100	3	4 kg	.5/sec	1 kg

TIP The M4 should be used for long-range sniping. Attach a 4X scope and you'll have one potent firearm at your disposal.

EXPLOSIVES

Quite a few *Spec Ops* missions call for you to destroy a building, vehicle, or some other piece of equipment. Explosives come in four categories.

⊕ Claymores   ⊕ Grenades

⊕ Rocket launcher   ⊕ Satchel charge

CLAYMORE AND CLACKER

The claymore is a remote-detonated, fragmentation antipersonnel mine with a 10-meter blast radius. The claymore is placed, and then detonated by pressing the clacker in your inventory. The strength of the claymore is the breathing room it offers. Unlike a satchel charge, you won't have to flee when you set this device down. It's especially useful in multiplayer games when you'd like to plant one in a sniper position. The second the sniper gets in position, press the clacker and kaboom—no more sniper.

GRENADES

Grenades can be either thrown by hand or shot forth with the M203 for increased distance. Some grenades explode with shrapnel while others send out a thick cloud of smoke to create a diversion or decrease your visibility to the enemy.

FRAG GRENADE

Frag grenades are antipersonnel explosives with a 3-meter kill radius against unarmored targets. Frag grenades are useful in clearing out a building, causing diversions, and taking out multiple enemies with a single blow.

Frag grenades should be used with care as they can bounce off trees and other objects if you're not careful. After throwing a frag grenade, quickly retreat and duck for cover unless you're absolutely sure the grenade is far enough away to prevent your receiving some critical damage.

HE GRENADE

The most powerful grenade in *Spec Ops* is the HE grenade. HE stands for high explosive, a claim backed up by the impressive 7-meter kill radius against armored targets.

In contrast to the frag grenade, *always* retreat after tossing the HE or risk losing your limbs.

SMOKE GRENADE

If you come under heavy fire and find yourself pinned down with nowhere to go, the trusty smoke grenade could help you. While the smoke grenade doesn't cause any damage, it can blind the enemy and at least obscure the view of you while you seek safety during the mayhem.

WHITE PHOSPHOROUS GRENADE

This grenade is all about carnage — it packs quite a punch with a 12-meter blast radius. Once this baby goes live, you'll have no choice but to go prone under cover or flee in the opposite direction. When the white phosphorous grenade finally explodes and strikes, the enemy will catch on fire and die a brutal death.

RPG7

Issued to forces of the former Soviet Union and North Korea, the RPG7 proved to be a very simple and functional weapon. It has an anti-vehicle/armor role and is also effective against fixed emplacements. Its effective range is thought to be approximately 500 meters when used against a fixed target and about 300 meters when fired at a moving target. Reportedly, it can penetrate 12 inches of conventional armor plate.

Weapon	Damage	Burst Count	Loadout Wgt.	Burst Delay	Clip Wgt.
RPG7	75	1	N/A	.6/sec	N/A

SATCHEL CHARGE

You'll be using the satchel charge quite a bit during your tour of duty to take out buildings, vehicles, and other enemy equipment. The key difference between a satchel charge and a claymore is that the satchel has a timer that must be set the moment it is dropped. The timer can be set anywhere from 1 second to a full 30 seconds. You should give yourself at least 8 seconds to flee from the satchel charge as it has a 20-meter blast radius that takes everything out within that range.

MACHINE GUNS

While assault rifles shine in long-range combat, machine guns have one single purpose: close-range combat. Their rapid fire rate and large capacity clips ensure that you'll be able to enjoy a long burst of bullets without the worry of constant reloads. On the downside, if you're targeted from long range, a machine gun won't help.

M249

The M249 is a lightweight, portable machine gun capable of delivering a large volume of effective fire to support infantry squad operations. The M249 fires the M855 improved NATO standard SS 109 type 5.56-mm ammunition. The M249 replaces the two automatic M16A1 rifles in the rifle squad on a one-for-one basis in all infantry-type units and in other units requiring high firepower. Fielded in the mid-1980s, the M249 filled the void created by the retirement of the Browning automatic rifle (BAR) during the 1950s because interim automatic weapons (M14 Series/M16A1 rifles) had failed as viable "base of fire" weapons.

If at least one member of your squad has an M249, you can rest easy when the enemy comes up close and personal. There's no better weapon than the M249 when you're being rushed by several opponents. Its lethal damage, short burst rate, and high number of bullets in a burst ensure that enemies will be quickly overwhelmed if they attempt to bring the fight to you. The drawback to the M249 (besides its inability to deal with a long-range threat) is that each clip weighs 4 kg, which doesn't leave much room for other equipment.

Weapon	Damage	Burst Count	Loadout Wgt.	Burst Delay	Clip Wgt.
M249	100	7	9 kg	.9/sec	4 kg

M60

The M60 series 7.62-mm machine gun has been the U.S. Army's general purpose medium machine gun since the late 1950s. The M60 fires standard NATO 7.62-mm ammunition and is used as a general support, crew-served weapon. It has a removable barrel that can be changed easily to prevent overheating. The weapon has an integral, folding bipod and can also be mounted on a folding tripod. The M60 series is now being replaced by the M240B 7.62-mm medium machine gun.

The glory days of the M60 are gone. In fact, you'll only be able to outfit the M60 for missions in Vietnam. On the plus side, there's no better tool for dealing with the hostile enemy in Vietnam than the trusty, rugged, damaging M60. Its short burst delay, mixed with extremely high damage, makes this a worthy weapon for close combat. If you're engaged by a long-range enemy, don't expect the M60 to be much help. Sit it out and wait for the enemy to come for you.

Weapon	Damage	Burst Count	Loadout Wgt.	Burst Delay	Clip Wgt.
M60	125	3	13 kg	.6/sec	3 kg

MP5 SD

The Heckler and Koch MP5 submachine gun is a lightweight, air-cooled, magazine-fed, delayed-blowback-operated, select-fire weapon that can be shouldered or handfired. It fires from a closed-bolt position in semiautomatic, two- or three-round bursts, and sustained fire modes. The weapon uses the unique H&K roller-locked bolt system, common throughout the H&K family of small arms. The unique features of the H&K MP5 submachine gun include a free-floating, cold hammer-forged barrel; stamped, sheet-steel receiver; fluted chamber; straight-line stock; and a pistol grip with ambidextrous safety/selector lever. The bare metal surfaces of the MP5 are phosphated and coated with black lacquer paint.

Weapon	Damage	Burst Count	Loadout Wgt.	Burst Delay	Clip Wgt.
MP5 SD	60	3	6 kg	.4/sec	1kg

RPK

After the 5.45-mm new cartridge and AK74 assault rifle entered service, the RPK74 light machine gun was developed from the rifle. The RPKS74 version with folding butt was intended for airborne paratroops. These machine guns differ from the AK74 assault rifle in barrel length and weight, sight windage mechanism, butt shape, dimensions weight, and the design of the recoil compensator.

Another tool of the enemy, the RPK doesn't have much going for it. A low damage rating and low burst count make this an ineffective weapon both at long and short range. Fortunately, none of this is your concern unless you happen to pick up one from a fallen enemy. While no match for anything you might already be carrying, the RPK can at least be a backup when your main weapon runs out of ammo.

Weapon	Damage	Burst Count	Loadout Wgt.	Burst Delay	Clip Wgt.
RPK	50	3	N/A	.5/sec	N/A

SCOPES

Scopes come in a wide variety and will prove to be among your best allies in beating the enemy. A sniper rifle without a scope is like a gun without a trigger. Before you enter combat, make sure you're loaded up with the proper equipment and have the right scope for the job.

2× AND 4× SNIPER SCOPE

The 2× sniper scope will double your visual range, and the 4× will quadruple it. Unfortunately, scopes cannot be fitted to just any weapon. You can attach the 2× and 4× scope to these weapons:

- AK74
- SSG
- G11
- M4
- BMP50

ACOG

The ACOG is an aiming dot illuminated by an amber filter. While it doesn't offer much in the way of magnification, it does make poor visibility more tolerable by cutting out the haze.

The primary strength of the ACOG is that it can be fitted to any weapon except the Ithaca, making it a great tool for any mission, night or day.

PART

I

If an enemy is close, you'll see the aiming dot of the ACOG appear on his body. At longer range, the dot will be difficult to see, but that doesn't mean you can't strike your target. A good strategy is to aim the dot at the ground, and then slowly lift your aim, using judgment, until you think you've got the site placed over the enemy.

AN/PAS-13

The AN/PAS-13 increases your visual range by a factor of 4. This thermal scope will make all heat-emitting objects turn white while the rest of your view turns red. This is especially useful when attempting to track the enemy under heavy foliage. The AN/PAS-13 can be attached to the following weapons:

- AK74
- SSG
- G11
- M4
- BMP50

AN/PVS-7B

The AN/PVS-7B increases your visual range by a factor of 4 and is used in conjunction with night-vision goggles. Taking an AN/PVS-7B into a night mission is a must if you plan to snipe the enemy. The AN/PVS-7B can be attached to the following weapons:

- AK74
- SSG
- G11
- M4
- BMP50

BINOCULARS

Binoculars are handy tools to survey the landscape from long distances. A pair of binoculars offers an increase in visual range far beyond the capability of any scope. Unfortunately, you cannot shoot a firearm while looking through binoculars.

SHOTGUN

There is no better weapon for close combat than a good, old shotgun. While a machine gun is an exceptional weapon for medium-range combat, it cannot compete with the lethal blast of a shotgun at point-blank range. Any Ranger in your squad outfitted with a shotgun will be a force to be reckoned with.

ITHACA 37

This 12-gauge shotgun is a manually operated (pump), repeating shotgun with ghost ring sights. The shotgun is for guard duty, prisoner supervision, riot control, or any situation requiring the use of a weapon in close quarters.

Having an Ithaca 37 in your inventory means you'll be ready for close combat. A single shot from this lethal weapon is enough to take out any enemy. The wide spread of the blast means you don't have to be very accurate when firing. The Ithaca 37 is a must for missions where you'll be infiltrating enemy structures.

Weapon	Damage	Burst Count	Loadout Wgt.	Burst Delay	Clip Wgt.
Ithaca 37	150	7	4 kg	.7/sec	2 kg

SNIPER RIFLES

A sniper rifle is a must on any mission. There's no better way to deal with enemies than to kill them before they know you exist. The prime directive of any Ranger is to avoid close combat at all costs. The only way to ensure that is to take out the enemy at long range with a sniper rifle, and then move in the recon team.

BMP50

This revolutionary .50 caliber semiautomatic rifle allows lone soldiers to destroy or disable sophisticated targets. Armored personnel carriers, radar dishes, communications vehicles, aircraft, and area submunitions are all vulnerable to its strike capability. With decisive force and without the need for the manpower and expense of mortar or rocket crews, forces can engage the opposition at distances far beyond the range of small-arms fire. Using standard armor-piercing and incendiary ammunition, this weapon has sophisticated long-range accuracy.

The BMP50 is the sniper weapon of choice, offering almost twice the damage of the SSG and a slightly faster burst delay. The main difference besides the damage is the critical 2 kg in weight difference—2kg that could be used for other equipment. If you're traveling light on a mission, take a BMP50 along for the ride. On the other hand, if you think you'll be mixing it up with the enemy or need to use an explosive charge, take a step back and settle for the SSG.

Weapon	Damage	Burst Count	Loadout Wgt.	Burst Delay	Clip Wgt.
BMP50	500	1	7 kg	1.2/sec	2 kg

SSG

The SSG is the Austrian Army's standard issue sniper rifle. The SSG69 is so accurate, it's won several international competitions. The ZF69 scope is graduated for firing out to 800 meters in distance.

As is evident in the chart, the SSG does one thing very well. Its brutal damage ensures that a single, well-placed shot will bring down a most determined foe. Be prepared for a long reload wait before popping off another shot. It is for that reason that the SSG must be handled with care. Every shot must count. One miss will alert the enemy to your location, and the delay between fire times could lead to the enemy retaliating before you can finish him off.

Weapon	Damage	Burst Count	Loadout Wgt.	Burst Delay	Clip Wgt.
SSG	300	1	5 kg	1.5/sec	2 kg

MISCELLANEOUS EQUIPMENT

Besides weapons and explosives, equipment and supplies help during a mission. These range from medkits to ammo boxes, most of which can be outfitted before a mission, while others can be found in the mission area.

 **Ammo box:** Contains clips for any gun.

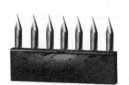 **Enemy ammo clip:** Contains a certain number of rounds, depending on the ammo type.

 **Flak vest:** Increases armor.

 **Medkit:** Increases health when you select medkit from your inventory list and press Enter.

PART II

Combat Tactics

Congratulations on passing basic training, soldier! You're now ready for the next and final phase of your education. Engaging in combat with the enemy will be an all too frequent occurrence and you had better be prepared. Before we let you loose on the battlefield, you'll need to be proficient in the use of the sniper rifle, explosives, squad commands, and general combat tactics. Once you're comfortable with the expectations of the U.S. Army Rangers, you'll want to take your abilities to the next level by engaging human opponents on the Internet. This last leg of your education will brief you on deathmatch combat, team play, and co-op strategies.

CHAPTER 4

Single-Player
Tactics

You've completed boot camp and drooled over the medley of available equipment. Now you're itching for a fight. Grabbing supplies and checking weapons, your partner and you venture out on a night mission, full of hopes and dreams. Three seconds later, you're both lying in pools of blood, mowed down by the faceless enemy you never knew.

Take your abilities to the next level if you want to win the wide variety of missions that compose the *Spec Ops* experience. Unlike in the bulk of first-person shooter games on the market, running into the thick of action in *Spec Ops* is a gateway to failure. *Spec Ops* demands strategy.

THE SEVEN DEADLY SKILLS

Chances are, if you dove into *Spec Ops*, you faced the cold reality of death before knowing what hit you. Throwing caution to the wind, you rushed the enemy. Your fellow Ranger was butchered while crossfire pinned you down. If nothing else, you sure looked valiant right before you died.

TIP   Impatience is guaranteed to kill you. Take the time to scout and explore before rushing into unknown territory.

If you plan your actions, study your surroundings, communicate with your partner, and monitor enemy activity, mission success is ensured. It's the hasty, impatient warrior who is weeded out of the military and into the cemetery.

Success in any mission depends on mastering seven skills.

1. Ordering your partner

2. Postures

3. Sniping

4. Situational awareness

5. Outfitting

6. Monitoring the GPS

7. Changing Rangers

ORDERING YOUR PARTNER

A partner accompanies you on every mission in *Spec Ops*. Work as a team to overcome the enemy's numerical superiority. How you work as a unit means the difference between success and failure. Figure 4.1 illustrates the result of poor teamwork.

You can issue four commands to your partner, and each command plays a vital role in the mission's outcome. Let's take a closer look at each command to see how best to use them.

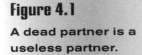

Figure 4.1

A dead partner is a useless partner.

MOVE UP

This command is often a lifesaver. If you've been playing *Spec Ops* and are often riddled with enemy fire, stem the flow by having your partner participate in the action.

TIP Use the Move Up command to scout enemy territory and set up offensive attacks.

When you issue this command, it tells your partner to move in the direction you're currently facing for approximately 30 feet (see Figure 4.2). Once he reaches the limit, he'll hunker down and await the next order.

While this command is useful for scouting, it can also be used to set up crossfire or check out locations either behind or at your sides. If you're confident the enemy is on the other side of a hill, it's dangerous to send your partner to the top. A better plan would be to look at one side of the hill and issue the Move Up command. This places him in a strategic yet secure location, so he's safe from potential crossfire attack, while you move to the other side of the hill.

WARNING When you tell your partner to Move Up—he'll do it. When he arrives at his destination, he won't open fire on visible enemies unless you tell him to do so.

Figure 4.2

Your partner scouts
the territory ahead.

FOLLOW ME

A crooked road disappears into the jungle ahead. Enemies could be waiting for a clear shot at you. Throwing caution to the wind, you move forward, keeping an eye out for signs of activity. Suddenly, machine-gun fire cracks through the air and tracer bullets bounce off nearby trees. You open fire but it's too late. The enemy rushes you. Your last ditch effort is to tell your partner to open fire. Unfortunately, he's nowhere near. Where is he? Most likely, he's back a 100 feet or so, cleaning his nails while you're being slaughtered, all because you didn't tell him to Follow Me.

This happens if you don't pay attention. Unless you issue the Follow Me command, your partner stands still while you move forward, putting the odds in favor of the enemy.

Follow Me when combined with Move Up are potent commands. When you explore new territory, your partner should follow close by your side. Ordering him to Move Up sends him trudging forward to check your current location.

FIRE 'EM UP

Using the above example, let's say your partner is close by your side and you spot the enemy. You open fire and the enemy rushes toward you, guns blazing. Unfortunately, your partner watches as you are riddled with bullets. Why isn't he firing? You haven't told him to Fire 'Em Up!

Remember, you're in charge of this unit, and, like the military, actions are carried out only when an order is given. While you might think your partner will grab his gun and help out in a moment of crisis, he's bound by his last order. If that order wasn't to open fire, he won't help.

TIP When you come under fire in *Spec Ops*, quickly issue the Fire 'Em Up command so your partner helps attack the enemy.

When your partner has been given permission to engage the enemy, he will scan in all directions and shoot anything that moves, as long as it is within range. This gives you plenty of opportunity to ready a new weapon or plant an explosive, knowing your partner will fire on any approaching enemy.

HOLD UP

This important order can serve several purposes, depending on what you want to do. Similar to the Fire 'Em Up command, this order will stop your partner from moving yet still give him permission to open fire on visible enemies.

TIP If you want to run ahead and leave your partner behind to act as a rear defense, issue the Hold Up command.

This order is perfect for setting up an ambush or crossfire. Here's an example. Let's say you're confident the enemy is approaching. The ultimate setup is for you to be on one side of the road and your partner on the other. Look in the direction you want your partner to hold and issue the Move Up command. When he reaches his destination, issue the Hold Up command and he'll stand his ground while opening fire on the first thing that moves (see Figure 4.3).

Figure 4.3

Your partner holds the ground on the other side of the road, ready to blow away any enemy who approaches.

COMMAND RECAP

Together, the above four commands are critical to master if you intend to be successful at *Spec Ops*. Just one minor slipup during the course of a mission can spell disaster. It's for this reason that you should take each mission slowly (unless pressed by a time limit) and ensure you know what you're doing every step of the way. You have a partner for a reason, and he should be used to the fullest extent possible. Not only will he protect your backside but he'll share in the hazard of scouting new territory and, more importantly, assist you in creating impenetrable defensive positions.

In most *Spec Ops* missions, you venture into enemy territory, slowly making your way toward the objective. If you plan to reach the objective in one piece, run through this checklist.

⊕ Always have your partner close by your side in case trouble starts.

⊕ Always give your partner the Fire 'Em Up command after a Move Up order.

⊕ Use the Hold Up command to keep your partner in one spot while you head somewhere else.

POSTURES

The posture of your Ranger can mean the difference between life and death. *Spec Ops* allows the player to stand up straight, crouch down, or lie prone. Each of these postures should be used often to prevent the enemy from putting bullets in you.

STAND

When you first begin a mission, your Ranger and partner will be in the stand posture, guns checked and ready to engage the enemy. Unfortunately, the stand posture is an invitation to death. You might as well paint a big, fat target on your head in enemy territory. If nothing else, the enemy will thank you for making it so easy to wipe you off the face of the Earth.

TIP Stand when you need a quick burst of speed.

The only benefit to the stand posture is speed. Your Ranger will move quickly, allowing you to get from point A to point B as rapidly as possible (see Figure 4.4).

WARNING Lobbing a grenade while in the stand posture propels it far.

Figure 4.4
Two standing targets

CROUCH

When you move into the crouch posture, you limit your visibility while still allowing for movement speed. Crouched movement is the middle ground when you need to be light on your toes and sneaky too (see Figure 4.5).

Figure 4.5
A crouched Ranger is tough to hit.

Placing your Ranger in the crouched posture will increase his accuracy while reducing the chance of his being seen by the enemy.

 **TIP** Crouch behind objects to reduce your exposure to the enemy.

The crouch posture allows you to duck behind just about any object in the game. When the enemy shoots, look for cover and crouch down. As long as you're not exposed, the enemy can't hit you. Of course, now that you're pinned down, you have other problems. How do you get out of this situation? Simple. Wait for the enemy to cease fire, quickly toggle to the stand posture, and fire a few quick bursts from your gun. If your aim is good, you'll wipe out the threat and continue with the mission.

 **WARNING** A grenade lobbed from the crouch posture lands about 30 feet away. Run in the opposite direction or you'll be nailed by the blast.

PRONE

The prone posture should be used more than any other. Not only does this posture allow for the best firing accuracy, but it also reduces the enemy's ability to see and hit you at the same time. Unfortunately, this comes at the expense of speed and mobility.

 TIP Any time the enemy fires, duck into a prone posture to reduce your risk.

The greatest strength of the prone posture is your new ability to crawl. By holding down the Shift key and moving, your Ranger will slowly (and quietly) crawl forward. This is a great posture when you're approaching an enemy from behind and you'd like to take him as quietly as possible (see Figure 4.6).

Having your Ranger in the prone posture allows you to roll to either side as well. Simply press the Strafe key and he'll tumble right or left without getting up. This is useful when you're pinned behind an object, and want to roll out quickly and fire off a few shots. With practice, the prone posture can be the most valuable skill you have.

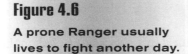

Figure 4.6

A prone Ranger usually lives to fight another day.

POSTURE RECAP

Use the three different postures as much as possible, depending on the combat situation you face. Whatever posture you assume, your partner will follow. For instance, if you're sending your partner to the top of a hill to investigate possible enemy activity, you'd better be in the prone position or he's going to be a sitting duck up there.

- **Stand:** Use stand only for quick bursts of speed.

- **Crouch:** Use crouch to hide behind objects and reduce your visibility.

- **Prone:** Use prone for sniping and sneaking.

SNIPING

The enemy will snipe you in a heartbeat so you might as well beat them to the punch. A key element to effective sniping is locating a solid position that gives you a clear view of your surroundings. This doesn't mean lying flat on your face in the middle of a road, but do use hills, foliage, and buildings to your advantage (see Figure 4.7).

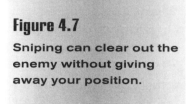

Figure 4.7

Sniping can clear out the enemy without giving away your position.

There are three ways to snipe the enemy in *Spec Ops*, depending on the gun you selected before the mission began.

2× OR 4× SCOPE

By far, the most accurate and deadly way to take out the enemy is by using a 2× or 4× scope. This allows you to pick them off from a distance while not giving away your current location. Simply press the Snipe key and a short list of available scopes will be indicated. Select either 2× or 4× (if available) and the perspective of the game will shift to a scope view. Now that you're in scope view, pan slowly until you see an enemy, line up the crosshair on the body part of your choice, and squeeze the trigger (see Figure 4.8).

Figure 4.8

This unsuspecting enemy is about to feel intense pain.

ACOG

The next best thing to using a 2X or 4X scope is the ACOG. You'll most likely use the ACOG more than any other add-on because it can be fitted to every weapon in *Spec Ops*. While it doesn't offer the accuracy or range of a 2X or 4X scope, it can still make the difference in the success or failure of your mission. Look at Figure 4.9 for an example of the ACOG.

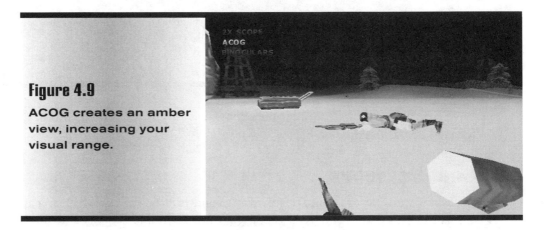

Figure 4.9

ACOG creates an amber view, increasing your visual range.

Best of all, ACOG allows you to move around the mission while still giving you a good idea of your nearby surroundings. Trying this with a 2X or 4X scope would be extremely dangerous because it limits your peripheral vision.

TIP It can be difficult to see the amber site of the ACOG at medium-to-long range. If you can see the enemy but can't site him, aim toward the ground until he comes into view. Carefully raise the ACOG again until you think you've lined up the enemy.

BINOCULARS

Binoculars are a good middle ground for the available scopes. If you're using binoculars, you don't have access to a 2X or 4X scope. On the other hand, the ACOG may not give you the visual range you need. What do you do? Whip out the binoculars and scan the area. Once you have sighted the enemy, put the binoculars away and power up the ACOG. Squeeze the trigger. That takes care of the enemy threat (see Figure 4.10).

TIP The binoculars are used to scan the horizon before moving into enemy territory.

Figure 4.10

Scan the horizon with your binoculars to locate the enemy.

SITUATIONAL AWARENESS

It helps to know what you're about to step into before you actually step in it. Running through a mission with little regard for enemy activity is a sure way to bring the mission to a quick end. *Spec Ops* is a game that demands you use your ears as well as your eyes.

If you're moving through a dense jungle, listen closely for enemy sounds. *Spec Ops* has a great sound system with real stereo panning, making it easy to figure out the direction of sound. When the gunfire starts, listen to its direction and proceed with caution.

TIP Let the enemy approach you, instead of approaching the enemy.

Unless you're pressed with a specific mission time, take your actions slowly. The enemy enjoys laying down booby traps and land mines. You will stumble upon them unless you pay attention (see Figure 4.11).

Figure 4.11
This land mine is about to go off and ruin what was otherwise a great day.

Situational awareness is more than just keeping your eyes and ears open for the enemy. Paying close attention to your current inventory, how many rounds are left in the clip, and what the status of your partner is all play an important role. If you're paying careful attention to all of these factors, you'll be at a big advantage over the enemy.

 **WARNING** If you trigger a land mine make sure you quickly get in the stand posture and run in the opposite direction! These devices have a very short fuse but can be avoided if you make haste.

OUTFITTING

You've wiped out most of the enemy. All that's left is to take out a few antiaircraft guns and call Starcom for pickup. Unfortunately, you're shy a satchel charge. Your only hope is to look around the enemy camp and hope to find an extra. If you don't, the mission is a wash and you failed because you didn't take the time to properly outfit your Rangers.

The only way to avoid this trap is to pay close attention to your mission objectives. If the mission calls for explosives, bring plenty along.

 TIP Try to give your partner an extra explosive if he can carry the extra weight.

While not having enough explosive power is a common error, not having the right gun for the job is another. The weapon you bring should be based on the objective you need to reach. If you'll be infiltrating an enemy base, your best bet is to bring a long-range weapon to pick off the enemy from a distance. If your job is to hold an area, then prepare for large numbers of the enemy moving in your direction. In this case, you'd need an automatic, such as the M60.

TIP Try not to outfit your Rangers with the exact same inventory. One Ranger should have the tools needed for long-range shooting while the other should have the firepower to handle matters up close and personal.

MONITORING THE GPS

The GPS (global positioning satellite) can be your best friend. Knowing the mission objective is one thing, but if you don't know how to get there, you're in big trouble. The GPS is always just a key away.

When activated, the GPS displays your current heading much like a compass. As you turn, it turns. At one point, you'll see a direction light up. This indicates you're heading toward the first waypoint for the mission. As long as the compass direction is illuminated, you're on the right track. If not, you're heading off the beaten path and may be lost.

Once the first event in a mission has been accomplished successfully, the GPS will automatically change to reflect the next waypoint. In this way, the GPS will always guide you in the correct direction (see Figure 4.12).

WARNING The GPS always leads you in a straight line from your current position to the next waypoint. While a straight line is always shorter, it isn't less dangerous. The GPS can lead you into exposure to enemy fire. Use the GPS as a guide, not as gospel.

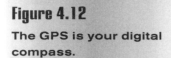

Figure 4.12
The GPS is your digital compass.

CHANGING RANGERS

Spec Ops players often overlook this command. It's true, you can play *Spec Ops* without ever jumping into the body of your partner, but those who take the time to make this command a part of their game style reap rewards.

Press the Tab key (or whichever key you've assigned) and you will see what your partner sees. Regularly swapping views gives you much better control over positioning your Rangers, especially when you want to set up an ambush.

Also, if your primary Ranger is injured, you can easily swap views with your partner, who stands a better chance of seeing the mission through to the end.

TIP Change your Ranger view when you send your partner on a scouting mission. Then, you'll be participating more in the action instead of hanging back and waiting.

CHAPTER 5

Deathmatch Strategy

Ranger Team Bravo allows up to eight players to battle each other in seven different environments. While the computer can put up a good fight, it is no match for human intelligence. That's where tactics are put to the real test. While a mission is a single-player or multiplayer game with a clear-cut objective, a level is the 3D environment where a mission/deathmatch takes place. Deathmatch strategies in this chapter will guide you through each of the seven levels and provide expert tips for dominating your opponent.

GENERAL DEATHMATCH STRATEGIES

There are winners and losers in computer gaming deathmatches where people from all over the world come together on the Internet to do mock battle with one another until one demolishes the other with guns, explosives, and snipers.

If you've played deathmatches before, you may have come across a player who never seems to lose. You try new ideas and change your style of play, but the result is always the same. You die. You lose.

Gentle Reader, it doesn't have to be that way. Not in *Spec Ops*. Unlike some other games, *Spec Ops* rewards patience and strategy. A sure way to die quickly is to treat *Spec Ops* like the average shooter, running around as fast as you can, shooting anything that moves, and hoarding health boxes. This tactic is an invitation to early death while your opponent mocks you in *Spec Ops* Chat. If you're tired of this happening to you, read on.

HEAD FOR THE HILLS

One sure way to be killed off regularly is to keep to the lower terrain. Chances are good your opponent stationed himself higher, whipped out a scope, and is locking crosshairs on your forehead (see Figure 5.1).

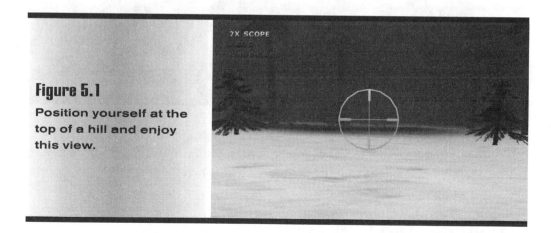

Figure 5.1

Position yourself at the top of a hill and enjoy this view.

The first priority at the beginning of any deathmatch level is to scout a high elevation and keep it to yourself. Find a spot that offers you the widest view possible while minimizing your exposure. Once you've found the perfect spot, take out your sniper rifle (or other long-range weapon) and scan the terrain until you sight the enemy. Press the trigger. The enemy will fall flat.

 WARNING Watch your back when looking through a sniper scope or your opponent could easily sneak behind you.

NEXT STOP, SECOND FLOOR

The majority of buildings on the deathmatch levels have more than one floor. It's more effective to be on the second floor, using the height advantage to increase your visual range. While you're staring out a window looking for the enemy, he could very well be sneaking in a rear door and shooting you in the back (see Figure 5.2).

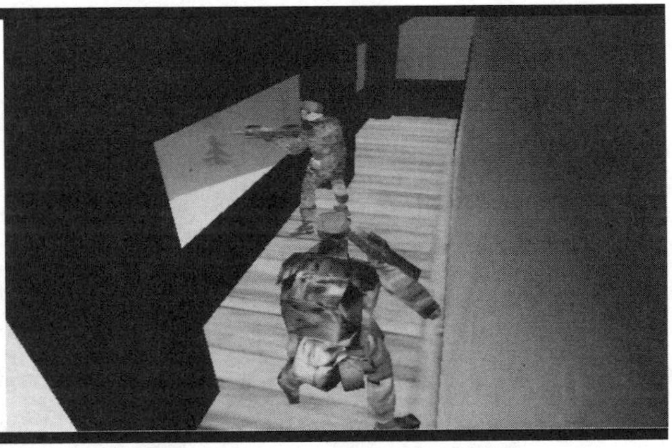

Figure 5.2
This inattentive sniper is about to learn a valuable lesson.

Protect your station by using your partner properly. Having your fellow Ranger stand in the same room as you doesn't help. On the lower floor, tell your partner Hold Up behind the building or near an exit. Then he could take out opponents strolling by.

UPROOT, DON'T ROOT

Holding the higher ground, positioning yourself on the second floor is a solid tactic for dominance, but you can't stay there forever. Sooner or later the enemy is going to wise up to what you're doing and take you out of action. Don't use the same tactic for too long. Move around, shake it up, keep the enemy on his toes. Just when he thinks he knows where you are, move off in the opposite direction and try something new. If you just killed the enemy from the second floor of a building, exit the building, skirt the border of the map, and find high ground. Confuse your opponent. Change tactics regularly. A confused opponent is a dead opponent.

 **TIP** Never stay in one spot for too long or the enemy will track you. Move around, mix it up, let them wonder where you are.

HUG A TREE

Trees are everywhere in *Spec Ops* and they do more than pump oxygen into the air and block sunlight. Trees block bullets for *Spec Ops* warriors. Simple as that. When approaching enemy territory, use the surrounding trees for cover (see Figure 5.3). Once you're down, roll to the right or left and quickly scan the area ahead. If the way is clear, pick a tree and move straight toward it. If done correctly, the enemy will never detect you coming.

Figure 5.3

A tree can make a big difference in living conditions.

GET DOWN, GET FUNKY

It's critical to use the postures in the single-player version of *Spec Ops* and it's even more so in multiplayer deathmatch. Unlike playing against a computer's artificial intelligence, which reacts to proximity, your opponent's eyes will see you, so don't run around a map while standing up. It's the equivalent of painting a big red target on your head. Instead, hunch down or crawl around the level, using the terrain and objects to disguise your movement. The lower you are, the more difficult it is to spot you.

Don't Panic!

You're crawling along the jungle floor and you suddenly hear the sound of a machine gun crackle through the air. Bullets rip into the ground around you and you feel panic. Because you're panicking, you're not thinking clearly. You begin to run in random directions and soon you are knocked out of action. What do you do when you come under fire? Stay calm. The worst is to lose your cool.

How do you handle a pressure situation? Scan the area and find the nearest hiding spot. It can be a tree, a bunker, a building. Don't stand and run, or chances are good you'll be gunned down before taking three steps. Remain in the prone position and roll toward your destination. This will keep you low to the ground while allowing you to move at a brisk speed. It's much faster than crawling.

Itchy Trigger Finger

You're in a comfortable sniping position, scanning the landscape for the first site of the enemy. Suddenly, your opponent comes into view and you get excited and squeeze off a few rounds. Now the enemy realizes he's under fire and will take evasive action. You blew your chance. Instead of firing at the first sign of foes, trail them with a scope, and fire when they stroll into an open area. When you strike in an open area, your opponent has nowhere to run. A patient Ranger waits until he knows he's going to nail his target.

Roll out the Barrels

There are several deathmatch levels with green barrels strewn around. These barrels contain a toxic nerve gas that, when struck with a bullet or explosive, will explode, killing anyone nearby (see Figure 5.4). While it's still more effective to kill someone with a bullet, it never hurts to bruise the ego by gassing them. If you die being gassed in a multiplayer game of *Spec Ops*, other players will laugh, and you will feel embarrassed. The gas takes a while to kill, whereas a bullet kills immediately. With gas, victims can still make a break for it, if they're fast. If you want to make sure you're going to kill someone, use a bullet. If you're near barrels, remember your opponent could booby trap the barrels too.

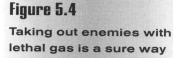

Figure 5.4

Taking out enemies with lethal gas is a sure way to humiliate them.

WARNING Shooting barrels can be hazardous to your health. If you unleash a toxic cloud, stay away from the area for a couple of minutes or you could be the next victim.

DIVERSIONARY TACTICS

One key to keeping the enemy on his toes is by flinging frag and gas grenades to make him think you're somewhere you're not. By lobbing a grenade in the opposite direction from which you're moving, the enemy is likely to think you're traveling the opposite way. Skirt around the border, approach the enemy from behind, and kill him.

FLYING ENEMIES

Outfit your deathmatch Ranger with at least one claymore or satchel charge. It will demoralize your opponent. Plant a claymore at a location you know the enemy likes to frequent and keep tabs on the spot. Once the enemy returns, press the claymore clacker and send him flying (see Figure. 5.5).

Satchel charges are a little trickier because of the timer. They can be useful when you know the enemy is following behind you. Give yourself five to eight seconds of leeway to get out of there, drop the satchel, set the timer, and run like a cheetah. If timed just right, your opponent will be no more.

Figure 5.5

Blowing up the opponent with a claymore

DEATHMATCH MAP STRATEGIES

Spec Ops: Ranger Team Bravo comes with seven deathmatch levels. Each will push your talents to the limit. Some take place in snowy terrain with poor visibility and others are in Iraq and Vietnam. Each map offers plenty of opportunities to use strategy, staking your claim to the highest hill or holding the bunker all to yourself. Some levels are large while others are compact. Each is a challenging experience.

Here's an overview of each deathmatch map and strategies to guide you toward victory.

Do Unto Others

Do Unto Others takes place on snow-covered Bosnian terrain with plenty of trees for cover. Each of the major compass points leads to a building. Some buildings can be climbed to the second floor and some serve only as cover.

DEFENSIVE POSITIONS

Do Unto Others has several hiding spots but nothing that will last you for very long. Since this map is small and compact, expect to find the enemy quickly. Your best bet is to head in one of four major directions until you find a house at the edge of the map. These houses will offer solid cover while giving you a good view of the nearby terrain.

SNIPER POSITIONS

The house at the south side of the map allows you to climb up to the second story where you can assume a sniping position (see Figure 5.6). This house is the key to the level and whoever holds it longest wins.

Figure 5.6

The house to the south is prime sniping real estate.

TIP Use your partner to monitor the house entrance while you snipe enemies.

GENERAL TIPS FOR DO UNTO OTHERS

- Be careful moving around the center of the map; you're a target from any direction and at long range.

- Use your partner to watch the southern entrance to the house if you're sniping from the second floor.

- To take out snipers, plant a claymore on the second floor of the house.

FRIENDLY FIRE

The Bosnian terrain on this level is cold with snow and packed with trees and buildings. In fact, there are so many buildings, you won't be at a loss for hiding and sniping spots. Neither will your opponents. While the number of places to hunker down is beneficial, if your opponent is sharp, this level can be challenging.

DEFENSIVE POSITIONS

At the south side of this level are several burned out buildings. One has a second floor accessible from a ramp. This is the only structure in the level with a second floor. It's a valuable position to hold. Use your partner to watch the sides of the building so he takes out approaching enemies.

Toward the northwest are a few toppled walls that will act as cover if you come under fire. To the northeast and north side of the map are dug out bunkers that, like the walls, provide cover (see Figure 5.7). Neither the walls nor the bunkers are perfect places to hide, but if you come under attack, you'll have little choice.

Figure 5.7

Use the bunkers to get out of sticky situations. If you kneel, your opponent in this bunker can't hit you.

SNIPER POSITIONS

The burned-out building to the south is the prime sniping spot, especially if you're mounted atop the second floor. Not only do you get plenty of coverage but you'll be able to see quite a bit of the terrain.

GENERAL TIPS FOR FRIENDLY FIRE

- Don't stay in one spot for long or the enemy will eventually track you.

- Secure and hold the two-story building at the south. It's valuable.

- Leave a claymore in the building to the south after you're done using it. It will be a nice present for whoever comes along next.

REINCARNATION

You've been sent back in time to fight your opponents within the choked jungles of Vietnam. Dirt roads bordered by towering trees snake in chaotic directions and lead to a grouping of thatched huts. The lack of sunlight makes your night-vision goggles a must and the hazy Vietnam air doesn't help your visibility.

DEFENSIVE POSITIONS

Any winding path will ultimately lead to an outcropping of huts. These huts are a perfect hiding spot to hold, but you need your partner's help to secure the area.

The huts provide defensive cover as long as you're crouched low and using the walls for cover. A better position is directly under a hut, on your stomach, blasting at anything that enters this area.

SNIPER POSITIONS

This is a difficult level to snipe in, as it seems no matter where you go or hide, you'll be exposed on at least onc of your sides. To pull off sniping, you need to use your partner to keep your six clear. While the central huts can be a challenge to snipe from (see Figure 5.8), hiding out in any one of the many pathways, preferably behind a bush or tree, is a better position. If you send your partner down the path behind you and have him Hold Up, he'll be able to fight off any attack from the rear.

Figure 5.8

These huts can be dangerous to approach, but once safely inside, do your best to hold them for yourself.

GENERAL TIPS FOR REINCARNATION

- Drop a claymore under a hut and blow up enemies hiding inside.

- Order your partner to watch the area behind you.

- Use bushes in the pathways for camouflage.

CRY HAVOC

Return to Vietnam where there's little sunlight and haze obscures your view. To make matters worse, the entire map is packed with objects, any one of which may be hiding an enemy. Perhaps the most interesting aspect of this level is the lack of any height advantage. You won't be able to climb up anything and put yourself in a good sniping position, so that alone makes this a challenging level.

DEFENSIVE POSITIONS

You'll find good defensive positions at every turn. Toppled altars, large towers (see Figure 5.9), boulders, and statues are yours for the asking. The massive temple complex is a great place to set up a crossfire as it allows for plenty of cover. By ordering your partner to one side or the other, you'll surprise the enemy the second he sets foot in this territory.

Figure 5.9

Be careful approaching these towers. You never know who is hiding behind one.

SNIPER POSITIONS

Sniping is difficult in this level and should be avoided unless your partner is watching your six. Since there are so many places to hide, your best bet is to set up ambushes by waiting for the enemy to walk by. Once he's safely past, open fire and mow him down.

GENERAL TIPS FOR CRY HAVOC

- Set claymores on the pathways near bushes. This will reduce the visibility of the object and give you a chance to blow up your opponent.

- Try to have your partner hide behind a large stone on one side of the road while you take the one opposite. You're set for a lethal ambush.

- Toss a grenade into the temple to weed out hidden enemies.

THERE CAN BE ONLY ONE

Strap on your desert gear and head to the mountainous region of Iraq in this interesting deathmatch level. You'll start from atop a mountain and will have to carefully make your way down and find cover quickly. This will be your first experience with toxic barrels and watchtowers, each of which could lead to victory or defeat.

DEFENSIVE POSITIONS

There's a wide assortment of great hiding spots in this level. Toward the southwest edge of the map is a large, metal bunker with gun slits on either side. You can't ask for a better spot than this. If you plant your partner outside the bunker and have him Hold Up it will be difficult for the enemy to reach you.

Beside the central mountain is a large storage shed full of boxes and barrels. If you intend to make this spot your station, push the boxes out of the shed so they don't cause you harm.

Two tall towers are at the east and west sides of the map. Both are prime camping spots for taking out the enemy.

SNIPER POSITIONS

You have two excellent choices for sniping in this level: the large metal bunker or up high in the tower. The advantage to the bunker is it is hard for the enemy to get to you if your partner is guarding the entrance.

The two towers give you the best view of the landscape, making it easy to scan the terrain in search of the enemy (see Figure 5.10). The only drawback to this position is the lack of cover from a sniper buried in the woods.

Figure 5.10
Sniping from the tower gives the best view of the area.

> ## GENERAL TIPS FOR THERE CAN ONLY BE ONE
>
> - Use either the bunker or one of the towers for your cover.
> - Have your partner watch the bunker entrance while you snipe.
> - Don't knock around barrels if you think the enemy is near because they make loud sounds and can give away your position.

DIAPER DAY

Once again you venture into Iraqi territory and attempt to overcome your enemy. Toxic barrels, huge towers, and several bunkers are hiding spots. Trees are everywhere, making this an excellent map to sneak and set up ambushes.

DEFENSIVE POSITIONS

Similar to There Can Be Only One, this map gives you plenty of options for covert activities. The ultimate key to protection is not rooting yourself in one spot, but going from bunker to tower to bunker to tower. Do this and the enemy will become flustered. Use your partner to monitor the stairs leading to the top of a tower so you're well protected (see Figure 5.11). Leave a claymore at the top and blow away a sniper who may be trying to pick you off.

Figure 5.11

The sniper atop this tower forgot to leave his partner on guard duty. He'll quickly realize the mistake.

SNIPER POSITIONS

The bunkers and towers are the best positions for sniping. While the bunker allows for extra protection in case of a rushing enemy, the tower gives the best view. If you're being hounded by a tower sniper, duck behind a bush, whip out your scope, and blow him away.

GENERAL TIPS FOR DIAPER DAY

- Shoot barrels when the enemy is near them and they'll die of toxic fumes.
- Let your partner guard the bottom of a tower while you camp up top.
- Leave a claymore in a bunker and blow it up if the enemy walks inside. Chances are, they won't notice it until it's far too late.

HILL OF THE KING

The most challenging deathmatch level is Hill of the King, deep in the heart of the Iraqi desert. You will find few structures to hide behind and will have to crawl over hills to lessen the risk. Most interesting is the massive, three-story tower at the center of the map. You'll find two sets of stairs leading to the top, plus several catwalks as you ascend. On the ground level, there is a land bridge connecting the tower to a moderate hill packed with crates, the only objects at ground level that offer decent hiding spots.

DEFENSIVE POSITIONS

There are few defensive positions on this map. You'll want to travel across the hills as carefully as possible, using as many trees as you can, and approach the tower at the center of the map. Whoever holds the tower will be the victor of this level, and it won't be easy. To hold the tower, order your partner to watch the ground floor or, better yet, the second-story catwalk. For an even more effective tactic, leave your partner on the other side of the land bridge, behind a crate (see Figure 5.12). When enemies advance, your partner will be there to take them out, unless you snipe them first.

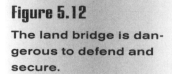

Figure 5.12

The land bridge is dangerous to defend and secure.

SNIPER POSITIONS

This level is all about the tower on the hill, the ultimate sniping position. The drawback is the tower is wide and you won't be able to see in all directions. As long as your partner is stationed somewhere on the ground or on a catwalk, you can be confident no one will sneak behind you.

If you are sniped from the tower, you'll have to make your way to the crates near the land bridge and try to snipe the enemy. This won't be easy if the enemy has been watching your advance. If nothing else, attempt to take out the enemy partner. Rush up the stairs for the kill.

GENERAL TIPS FOR HILL OF THE KING

- Whoever holds the tower wins the level. Simple as that.
- Use the crates for cover while approaching the tower.
- Keep your partner on the lower levels to protect your six.

CHAPTER 6

Co-op and
Team Tactics

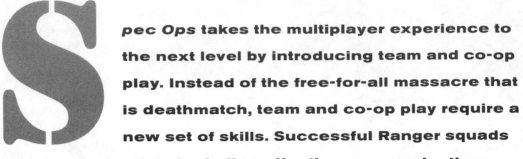

Spec *Ops* takes the multiplayer experience to the next level by introducing team and co-op play. Instead of the free-for-all massacre that is deathmatch, team and co-op play require a new set of skills. Successful Ranger squads will use new tactics, including effective communication, power formations, proper outfitting, and most importantly, premission planning.

You and several friends will work together in co-op play to take on the computer in any one of the available single-player missions. Team play puts you in either a defensive or offensive mode, using single-player missions from the game. One team will be the enemy— and will have computer controlled reinforcements—while the outnumbered Rangers must overcome daunting odds. You're in for the fight of your life.

CO-OP AND TEAM PLAY BRIEFING

If your Ranger partner has let you down in the thick of combat, try the co-op experience. You'll still have the support of your Ranger partner, but you'll also have at least one more human-controlled Ranger and his partner to help. Doubling the size of your force doesn't mean the mission will be easier. With more people in your squad, be sure to assign a proper role to each Ranger before the conflict begins.

PREMISSION PLANNING

Prior to starting a co-op or team mission, discuss with your fellow Ranger which mission to begin. Once you agree, it will be much easier to select the proper equipment.

Discuss the role each of you will play. Without getting this straight, you run the risk of entering the mission with redundant equipment that won't serve your goal. For instance, one squad should take on the role of recon and heavy firepower while the other concentrates on long-range sniping and explosives. By blending abilities, you'll be prepared for any situation.

For a two-player co-op game, your squad should consist of these preset Rangers for best results:

⊕ Grenadier

⊕ Recon

⊕ Sniper

⊕ Machine Gunner

TIP Zombie Games' official *Spec Ops* server is the best place to coordinate before a mission. Select Multiplayer and you will automatically connect to Zombie's proprietary server, which is not accessible by browser.

COMMUNICATION

Effective communication makes or breaks a mission. In a single-player game, you order your Ranger partner around with four basic commands. With the addition of another human partner, you'll have to increase communication or suffer consequences. Having extra members doesn't mean a team or co-op game is going to be a breeze. Having more people means the enemy has more targets.

EFFECTIVE CHAT COMMANDS

While you can still control your Ranger partner with the four commands—Hold Up, Move Up, Fire 'Em Up, and Follow Me—you'll have no direct control over your teammate and his partner. Instead, you must use the chat feature of multiplayer *Spec Ops* to lead you toward victory. It's easy to overlook the chat feature when the mission begins because you don't want to take precious time to type something. However, by using the following list of short commands, you can increase the effectiveness of your communication.

Command	What It Means
TG	Toss grenade.
E12, E3, E9, E6	Enemy ahead, right, left, behind.
CM	Cover me.
S12, S3, S9, S6	Sniper ahead, right, left, behind.
SH	Sniper high.
SL	Sniper low.
GD	Get down!
AC	Area clear.
MU	Move up, the area is clear.
M12, M3, M9, M6	Move ahead, move right, move left, move back.
C-(target)	Claymore target.
S-(target)	Place satchel charge near target.
NVG	Use night-vision goggles.
SFI	Search for items.
R12, R3, R9, R6	Recon (scout) ahead, right, left, behind.
SOS	Under fire!
SB	Secure building.
HB	Hold building.

PB	Pull back!
F3, F6	Flank enemy right, left.
LM	Land mine spotted!
RPD	Ranger partner dead!

TIP Use these commands often and they'll soon become second nature. Effectively communicating with your teammates will give you an advantage over the enemy.

FORMATIONS

Once you enter the mission, it's time to get to work. You should know exactly the role each member on your side will play and the mission objective. To see the mission through to the end, get into proper formation, or the enemy will mow you down.

ADVANCING FORMATION

One member of the team should assume the role of Recon. The player should take over the Recon Ranger and scout the area ahead (see Figure 6.1). Once this player has determined the area is clear and free from enemy fire, he should tell the rest of the squad to move up by saying, "AC."

Instead of moving as one big pack, have each of the advancing Rangers fan out. Send the Ranger partners ahead, followed by actual players. Have one person take the right side of the formation while the other takes the left. Continue moving forward in this fashion until you reach your mission objective.

TIP Advance carefully when nearing enemy territory. One false step could expose your entire team.

Figure 6.1

This Recon Ranger confirms the way is clear before calling the rest of the squad forward.

AMBUSH FORMATION

Set up an effective ambush when you see the enemy on the move. Determine the direction they're heading and what the intended destination might be. Once confident in this information, one team should flank to the right while the other heads left. Cut off the enemy advancement by nailing them from both sides at once. Make sure you have plenty of cover before launching the ambush; you never know if the enemy is setting you up (see Figure 6.2).

WARNING Try to keep the use of heavy explosives to a minimum when engaged in ambush. A stray grenade could spell doom for your teammates.

Figure 6.2

Carefully hidden Rangers will allow you to strike without the enemy spotting you.

INFILTRATION

Approaching an enemy structure is dangerous. You never know if the enemy is hidden away inside or monitoring the area from afar. For this reason, never approach a building with your entire team. Instead, send the Recon to investigate. When the Recon determines the area is clear, he can order the rest to move up and secure the building. With the area secure, you can set up an effective watch by leaving a Ranger partner behind a nearby obstacle to alert you to any enemy advance.

TIP There's no substitute for lobbing a grenade when you wish to clear a building of enemy activity.

BATTLE PLAN

It's too easy to lose your head when the fighting starts. Just when you think everything in your squad is nicely organized, a sudden outburst of bullets can cause havoc. As the saying goes, "The best laid plans often go awry." Even more so in *Spec Ops*, where the sudden outburst of gunfire can lead to a lapse in strategic thinking.

WHEN CHAOS STRIKES

Sooner or later, you're going to come face to face with a sticky situation. The enemy may have pinned you down or may have set you up with an ambush. When this occurs, it's easy to lose your cool and begin firing at anything that moves. Unfortunately, this is a great way to take casualties from enemy fire. When all heck breaks loose, take cover first and quickly assess the situation. Resist the temptation to use grenades and claymores, as this may cause more damage to your personnel than to the enemy.

TIP If you see your teammates pinned down by enemy gunfire, flank the opponents and take them out from behind.

One sure way to decrease your effectiveness as a unit is to concentrate your fire on a single enemy. Not only does this waste the bullets of everyone involved, it also gives the enemy a chance to nail you from the sides or behind. If it looks like your partner or teammate has the situation under control, move out carefully and make sure no enemies are nearby.

WARNING Killing a teammate by accident will cost you one point.

INDEPENDENCE

When taking cover, try not to position yourself near your partner or teammate (see Figure 6.3). Your objective is to stay as far apart as possible while still allowing for mutual support. The reason is simple. If you have more than one Ranger hiding behind a wall and a grenade happens to go off, you're both dead. It's far more effective to lose just one Ranger than your entire squad. Sometimes you will have little choice because of an enemy ambush. When this happens, deal with the situation quickly. Separate to lessen your exposure to risk.

Figure 6.3
Keeping your Rangers separated gives the enemy two targets instead of one.

WARNING Don't hide behind the same cover as your friends, or you could all be wiped out by one well-placed grenade or hidden claymore.

GUARD THE SNIPER

If your teammate is engaged in sniping, especially when perched in a building, it will be far more effective for you to personally guard him instead of having his Ranger partner do so. While the Ranger partner is good at dealing with a problem when it happens, he isn't so great at preventing it in the first place.

While your teammate is sniping, use the opportunity to scout the nearby area and ensure that the way is clear of enemies who may be trying to sneak in the back way. If possible, leave your Ranger partner on the outskirts of the sniping zone so he'll deal with any advances before the enemy gets to you. If done correctly, the sniper will have plenty of opportunity to get off quality shots, knowing he's protected from surprise ambush.

PART

II

PART III

Mission Walkthroughs

Listen up Rangers! So, you've completed Basic Training and made it through the grueling Combat Tactics courses. Don't be too proud of yourself just yet. You think you're ready for field action? First stop is the armory to stock up on weapons and gear. Take care in those selections, men. Stocking an Ithaca on a mission where you need long-range firepower could mean your mom will be receiving one of those letters. Once stocked, you'll be heading into hostile territory to begin your tour of duty. Fortunately for you scrubs, our intelligence division has obtained detailed walkthroughs for each of your forthcoming missions. You'll know what weapons to take, where flak vests are located, directions to all your objectives, how to survive what seem like impossible odds, and much more. As your commanding officer, I order you to use these walkthroughs to ensure your safety and the successful completion of the missions.

CHAPTER 7

Russia—
The Voronye Forest

A reconnaissance plane, the *Aurora*, was deployed over the Barents Sea to collect imagery of a Russian sub fleet massing in the Murmansk Sea. The United States lost contact with the *Aurora*. A beacon indicates the *Aurora* crashed somewhere in the southern region of the Voronye Forest. Both the United States and Russia have sent troops to locate the downed aircraft. In the first operation, the Ranger team must infiltrate an enemy tactical operations center to destroy a radio and knock out communications. With the enemy crippled, the Ranger team can recover the Starlos data module from the *Aurora*. The Rangers then advance to the landing zone and board the extraction helicopter. Two antiaircraft guns must be eliminated before the helicopter can be deployed.

MISSION 1—PHASE 1

⊕ **Situation:** The enemy has established a tactical ops center to secure the *Aurora* crash site. Enemy troops are reinforcing by truck transport.

⊕ **Mission:** Raid the enemy tactical center.

⊕ **Execution:** Destroy the troop truck moving down the road. Clear the road of enemy troops. Destroy the enemy radio in the tactical ops center. Radio SOCOM HQ when the mission is accomplished.

SQUAD SELECTION

For Mission 1—Phase 1, your best bet is to go with firepower, as opposed to excessive explosives. According to your briefing, you only need two heavy explosives to complete the task. You'll be facing tides of enemy troops. You're going to need extra bullets so outfit your two-man squad as follows:

⊕ **Ranger One: Rifleman**—M4 with 2X scope, three frag grenades, two claymores, two satchels, one medkit.

⊕ **Ranger Two: Machine Gunner**—M249, two frag grenades, two claymores, one satchel.

TACTICAL PLAN

Switch on your night vision goggles and take in the surroundings. Enemy troops will bear down on you within moments. Switch on your GPS to gain your heading.

This mission requires you to follow a dirt road into the enemy camp. Along the way you will intercept the supply truck, which you must destroy to complete the mission.

TIP Following the road can be tricky when you're wearing night goggles. Momentarily flick off the goggles to get a better view of the landscape, or follow the tire tracks, which indicate you are on the road.

Follow the road east and be sure to use your other Ranger as specified in the earlier chapter on single-player tactics. A partner trailing too far behind will expose you to excessive fire. Often two or even three enemies will spot you at once. If you are the only Ranger in sight, expect to be their sole target. The key to this mission is situational awareness. Enemies will hide behind trees and hills on the opposite side of the road. Move forward slowly, picking off enemies as you progress.

Follow the winding road and you'll eventually see the supply truck. There are several ways to destroy the truck, some more risky than others. Here are just a few of the ways you can complete your first mission objective:

 Quick attack: When the truck appears in front of you, fire at it. The truck will park for around 10 seconds. Enemy soldiers will pour from the truck's rear. Take them out quickly. If the truck restarts and continues down the road, fire again. When the truck stops, drop a claymore next to it (see Figure 7.1). Retreat and use the clacker to detonate your bomb. The alternative is to toss a grenade at the truck, although the accuracy factor makes this more challenging.

Figure 7.1

Destroying the supply truck with the claymore

 Intercept: Turn 90 degrees south and head over the hill. Once you begin to descend, you'll see a light station and the dirt road ahead. You are now in front of the truck. Place a claymore in the center of the road; get back to the hill and wait until the truck approaches and drives over the bomb. Use the clacker to blow up the truck.

 Stall: If you aren't ready to rush the truck at the start, concentrate on enemy soldiers surrounding the road. Eventually you will catch up to the truck. Fire at the truck to stop it, and then demolish it by tossing a claymore.

WARNING Be careful approaching the truck from the front. If you get flattened, you'll need a medkit to restore your health.

Continue to follow the road and you'll come to a fork. Keep to the right; the left path leads through a valley overflowing with enemies. Follow the right path south and west. When you approach the parked truck, the enemy camp is only a few steps away. The camp is filled with soldiers. Take your time picking them off. Three structures occupy the base camp with the radio toward the east side. Raid the other tents to get a flak vest and a medkit, and then take out the radio with either a frag grenade or a claymore (see Figure 7.2).

Figure 7.2

Your final objective: taking out the radio station

PART

III

MISSION 1—PHASE 1 DEBRIEFING

- Switch on your night vision goggles and the GPS immediately.

- Destroy the truck with an explosive. A rifle shot would merely persuade the soldiers to emerge from the truck's rear canopy.

- Search the light stations and dead soldiers for frag grenades, ammo clips, and medkits.

- Snipe enemy soldiers who are hiding behind trees and hills along the sides of the road.

- Follow the road to the right when it forks.

- The radio is in the east-most tent.

- Destroy the radio with a grenade or a claymore.

MISSION 1—PHASE 2

Situation: Enemy troops have secured the *Aurora* and established a defensive perimeter. SOCOM HQ has provided a key for the recovery of the Starlos data module.

Mission: Secure the crash site and recover the Starlos data module.

Execution: Clear all enemies from the crash site. Remove the Starlos module from the nose of the *Aurora*. Demolish the *Aurora* cockpit with a satchel charge. Radio SOCOM HQ when you've accomplished the mission.

SQUAD SELECTION

After demolishing their tactical base, it's time to make sure the enemy does not take control of the *Aurora*. Orders are to reach the *Aurora* cockpit, retrieve a data module, and destroy what's left of the aircraft. You need one explosive to take out the *Aurora*'s cockpit. This area is crowded with enemies, so significant rifle power is a must. Outfit your squad as follows:

⊕ **Ranger One: Rifleman**—M4 with 2✕ scope, three medkits, one satchel, two frag grenades.

⊕ **Ranger Two: Machine Gunner**—M249, one satchel, two extra clips.

TACTICAL PLAN

Use the night vision goggles frequently during this mission, much like the last, to get a bearing on charging enemies. Switch them on, as well as your GPS, immediately. Turn to the northeast and head toward an abandoned truck and a light station. Order your partner to follow. Gather the medkit, machine gun ammo, and the extra satchel next to the truck.

TIP Switch to Ranger Two, who does not have a medkit, and have him pick up the medkit.

Next, turn north and see what's left of the Aurora. Its flaming wreckage litters the valley. Follow the wreckage due north. Eventually you will come to the fuselage and cockpit of the downed reconnaissance aircraft.

TIP Stay to the east side of the *Aurora* wreckage. This way you'll only have to deal with one set of enemy soldiers. The west side of the ravine also contains armed enemies. Instead of confronting them at close quarters, snipe at them from a distance.

Keep following the wreckage due north until you reach the cockpit. For this mission you need the data module key. Order your Ranger partner to Fire 'Em Up while you insert the key into the cockpit and retrieve the data module.

TIP When using the data module key, don't stand in front of the *Aurora*'s cockpit. Stand to the left or the right. You can get hurt standing too close to the blown-off cockpit.

After you have the data module, drop a satchel charge next to the nose of the *Aurora* (see Figure 7.3) and set the timer for 30 seconds. Order your partner to follow and get as far away as you can, taking cover behind the *Aurora*'s tail end or foliage.

Figure 7.3

Saying goodbye to the
Aurora

WARNING Don't dally too close to the satchel. The blast radius is extreme and will more than likely kill you or your Ranger partner.

With the *Aurora* destroyed, enemy foot soldiers begin coming out of the forest in teams. Keep steady, using *Aurora* wreckage as cover and take out each and every soldier, using your remaining medkits as necessary. Radio HQ and it's on to the next phase.

MISSION 1—PHASE 2 DEBRIEFING

- Switch on the night vision goggles and the GPS.

- Head northeast to collect extra ammo, a medkit, and a satchel.

- Move cautiously due north, following the wreckage. Stay on the east side to avoid excessive enemies.

- Use the data module key on the *Aurora*'s cockpit.

- Collect the data module and place a satchel adjacent to the *Aurora*'s nose.

- Retreat back to the south and take out enemy stragglers.

MISSION 1—PHASE 3

⊕ **Situation:** An SOS Pavelow helicopter is en route for extraction.

⊕ **Mission:** Secure the landing zone and leave (exfiltrate) with the Starlos.

⊕ **Execution:** Locate the landing zone with the GPS. Destroy anti-aircraft guns defending the area. Clear the landing zone of enemy forces. Locate and board the helicopter for extraction.

SQUAD SELECTION

The goal is to destroy two antiaircraft guns positioned in front of the landing zone. Use two heavy explosives. Any explosive—a grenade launcher, a claymore, a satchel—will serve the purpose just fine. A Grenadier is especially helpful during this mission, as he can destroy the antiaircraft guns from a distance while the other Ranger lays cover fire. Outfit your soldiers as follows:

⊕ **Ranger One: Grenadier—**M16 with M203, 2× scope, two satchels, one medkit.

⊕ **Ranger Two: Rifleman—**M4 with 2× scope, three medkits, one satchel.

TACTICAL PLAN

The mission begins deep inside a valley, surrounded by impenetrable mountains. To get to the landing zone, you must head due east, straight through this valley, which enemy soldiers have overrun. Another problem you will face is booby traps littering the area. One step in the wrong direction and the helicopter could be leaving without you—and the *Aurora* data module.

Switch on your night goggles and GPS and head east. Plenty of trees line the valley, perfect for cover against the well-hidden enemies and useful to get first sight on charging foes. Be sure to watch your back; as you move forward through the valley, enemies will begin appearing from the rear. Move slowly and keep an eye on the ground for the land mines, placed in the center of the valley. A warning will announce if you have tripped a mine.

TIP Land mines are hidden in the center of the valley. Move through the valley by hugging either the northern or southern mountain face to avoid the booby traps. If you spot a mine, use a sniper scope to detonate it from a distance.

Soon you will come to two antiaircraft guns. You must destroy them before you are able to radio the extraction helicopter. When you approach the antiaircraft guns, enemies will begin charging from all sides. The guns won't fire at you. Use them for cover against the enemy squads (see Figure 7.4). After eliminating the surrounding forces, it's time to take care of the antiaircraft guns.

Figure 7.4
Using antiaircraft guns as cover is one key to Phase 3 success.

There are several ways you can destroy the antiaircraft guns. Each requires a type of heavy explosive:

⊕ **Satchel:** A satchel charge placed next to the antiaircraft gun will eliminate the gun in a hurry. Since it takes several seconds to position and set the timer on the satchel charge, it's best to rid the surrounding area of enemies before proceeding.

⊕ **Claymore:** A claymore mine will complete the objective just fine. Place a claymore next to one of the gun placements. Load up the claymore clacker in your inventory and set the mine off from a safe distance. Eliminate any nearby forces first.

TIP A claymore needs to be placed facing the target for it to be most effective.

⊕ **Grenade launcher:** The M203 grenade launcher is a quick and easy way to destroy the two antiaircraft guns. The safest way is to order your Ranger to Fire 'Em Up so he'll fire at any oncoming enemies on sight. Then, from a conservative distance, fire the M203 at each antiair gun. It's time to move on to the landing zone.

WARNING It may take several M203s to take out a target because they inflict the least damage. You can also try a grenade, but grenades are more difficult to accurately place.

With the two enemy guns out of action, pick up the extra medkit next to the light station. Move southeast, taking note not to move up on any portion of the mountain side. The extraction helicopter will land in the valley, next to the southern mountain. Enemies hiding behind trees abound in this area. Move forward cautiously, ordering your Ranger partner to fire at enemies on sight. Use the trees for cover as you follow the valley to the southern mountain. When you arrive, radio HQ and HQ will deploy the helicopter. Enter the helicopter to complete the *Aurora* mission.

PART

III

MISSION 1—PHASE 3 DEBRIEFING

- Switch on your night goggles and GPS.

- Follow the valley due east, staying close to either the northern or southern mountain to avoid land mines.

- Destroy the antiaircraft guns with satchel charges, claymore mines, or the grenade launcher.

- Use the forest for cover, heading southeast to the landing zone.

- Radio HQ to call in the extraction helicopter.

CHAPTER 8

North Korea—
Kapsan Missile Base

North Korea has been testing extended range Scud missiles. The *SSN Seawolf* has recovered one of these missiles in the East China Sea. The *Seawolf* investigated and determined that the Korean Scud shows signs of a chemical weapons payload. Surveillance turned up a heavily guarded facility in Kyongsong, and HQ sent a reconnaissance team to investigate. The reconnaissance team located a chemical weapons plant with four Scud C Tels missiles inside. HQ dispatches a 2/75 Ranger team to infiltrate the plant and eliminate the chemical weapons.

MISSION 2—PHASE 1

⊕ **Situation:** Chemical complex forces are on high alert. The enemy is patrolling the perimeter in small teams. A quick reaction force is patrolling the south west of the base bridge.

⊕ **Mission:** Demolish the bridge and air defense radar.

⊕ **Execution:** Disable the alarm in the second guard shack by grenade attack. Demolish the bridge by satchel charge. Demolish the radar by satchel charge. Radio HQ when the mission is complete.

SQUAD SELECTION

To complete all the tasks in this mission, equip yourself with at least three heavy explosives. Targets of opportunity include two guard towers, the radar, and the bridge. A Sniper is especially effective on this mission because many enemies are standing at guard posts or base camp gates. A prime squad selection should include:

⊕ **Ranger One: Sniper**—SSG with 4X scope, two medkits, one satchel.

⊕ **Ranger Two: Grenadier**—M16 with M203, two satchels, two grenades, four extra clips.

TACTICAL PLAN

This mission requires you to follow orders and to switch between your two Rangers. Fortunately, you're operating in daylight so night vision goggles aren't necessary. Turn on your GPS and head northwest, following the snow-covered road. You'll see a sign up ahead; turn left at the sign and there's the first enemy guard post.

Use the trees on the left side of the road for cover and pull your Sniper up front. Use the 4X scope and take out the two enemies guarding the exterior of the guard post. Select the other Ranger and move up ahead, ordering the Sniper to Hold Up. Another enemy is waiting on the other side of the guard post. Kill him quickly. Face northwest and take out any other enemies approaching from the road.

Although it isn't necessary to complete the mission, you can use a satchel charge to destroy this guard post.

WARNING This road rests on the side of a cliff. Beware the drop to the northeastern side. If one of your Rangers falls off the cliff, you could have a difficult time recovering and reaching the road again.

Hug the left side snow bank and you'll see a cliff above you. Some enemies might attempt to fire at you from that vantage point. Remove them with your Sniper. On top of this snow bank is the second guard post. It houses the alarm. Switch to your Grenadier and destroy the guard post with the M203 grenade launcher (you will need to be in ACOG mode). If you have trouble using the grenade launcher against this structure, maneuver up the snow bank and eliminate the post with a satchel charge. After you destroy the guard post, take advantage of the flaming remains as cover against nearby enemies.

TIP Alternatively, you can continue northwest on the path where you destroyed the first guard post. The road swings around and you can enter the camp from there, avoiding the climb up the snow bank.

From the second guard post and facing south, you will spot two enemies guarding one of the entrances to the camp. Use your Sniper to eliminate them (see Figure 8.1). You are now free to charge into the base camp; your first target is the radar dome in the center of camp.

Figure 8.1

The 4X scope and the SSG make quick work of enemy guards.

Enemies swarm the camp but there's plenty of cover in the barracks, generators, and trucks. Don't use the barrels as cover because they'll explode if shot. Move your Ranger team to the radar dome and order your partner to Fire 'Em Up so he shoots at enemies on sight. Place a satchel charge next to the radar dome, set the timer for 30 seconds, and move back behind one of the structures.

TIP To the southwest edge of the base is a small barracks where you'll find a medkit and a flak vest.

The bridge is your final target. From the radar dome, head northwest to move through another gate, exiting the base camp. This road leads through a forest and ends with the bridge you must destroy. Don't use the truck in the middle of this road for cover. Well-hidden enemies fill the forest and if you hide beside the truck, they'll quickly mow you down. Enter one side of the forest and eliminate the enemies hiding among the trees. Once the area is clear, move onto the bridge and place a satchel charge. Set the timer to 30 seconds and retreat to a safe distance. Radio Starcom to end the mission.

MISSION 2—PHASE 1 DEBRIEFING

- Use the Sniper on the guards at the gate.
- Destroy the second guard post with the grenade launcher or a satchel charge.
- Use the barracks inside the base for cover.
- Destroy the radar dome with a satchel charge.
- Don't use the truck near the bridge as cover.
- Take out the enemies remaining in the forest near the bridge.
- Remove the bridge with a satchel charge.

PART

III

MISSION 2—PHASE 2

- ⊕ **Situation:** A nearby squadron of MIG-23 aircraft defends the weapons complex. Enemy ground crews are on standby alert to defend the MIGs from attack.

- ⊕ **Mission:** Raid the airbase and destroy the MIGs.

- ⊕ **Execution:** Recon the airbase. Clear the area of enemy forces. Demolish the MIGs by satchel charge. Radio HQ when the mission is complete.

SQUAD SELECTION

Enter this mission at a well-guarded gate to the base camp and airfield. A Sniper is a wise choice for this mission because you can safely eliminate most of the bad guys from the gate without putting yourself in danger. You need at least three satchels to complete this mission. You can find additional satchel charges inside the base. Select the following squad:

- ⊕ **Ranger One: Sniper**—SSG with 4X scope, IR scope, one medkit, one satchel.

- ⊕ **Ranger Two: Rifleman**—M4, 2X scope, one medkit, two satchels, two grenades.

TACTICAL PLAN

Take the infrared scope with you on this mission, along with the Sniper, because the mission begins at a heavily guarded gate. Quietly and efficiently kill all the guards with your Sniper. Order your Ranger to Hold Up until all visible guards are terminated. Move cautiously into the gate area, heading north and taking cover by the two barracks. As you move into position, fire at enemies that peek out from the trees or from behind the structures. Extra items are on the ground, next to the barracks. You'll find a HE grenade, some ammo, and two satchels. Another satchel is east of this position.

Move into the base. Watch closely the canopy tents to the north-northwest. Since enemies are hiding behind mounds and sheds, seek cover inside the nearest canopy. Kill any soldiers inside, and use the Sniper to eliminate any rushing enemies from a distance. Move to the canopy to the north of your current position and take cover once again. Remove any enemies you spot outside.

Head west outside this tent and pick up the road leading northwest and to the airfield. There is plenty of cover along this road, including a tent and additional mounds, but there's also danger. You'll be coming under fire. Make frequent stops to dispose of any enemies who impede your path. Soon you will come across a bunker protecting an enemy sniper. Take him out from a distance with your Sniper's IR scope. You can pick up another satchel inside the bunker.

The airfield and four MIGs are just to the north. Head up to the runway and locate the first MIG, which appears to be ready for take off (see Figure 8.2). Place a satchel charge by the MIG, set the timer, and take cover behind the sheds to the south.

Figure 8.2

Destroying the first MIG

PART

III

Get the enemy's attention by demolishing the first MIG. Charging down the runway could be dangerous since there's no protection against enemy fire. Hug, instead, the southern-most fence, which just happens to be where the enemy has parked additional MIGs. While using the remaining MIGs for cover, terminate the enemy forces charging across the runway. Place satchel charges next to each MIG as you make your way to the fourth and final one. When you've destroyed all the MIGs, call for extraction on the SATCOM radio.

MISSION 2—PHASE 2 DEBRIEFING

- Use your Sniper and IR scope against the gate guards.

- Collect the satchel charges and ammo near the gate.

- Take cover inside the tents.

- Move to the airfield, taking cover behind mounds and sheds.

- Destroy the first MIG with a satchel charge.

- Hug the southern fence, avoiding the center of the runway.

- Use satchel charges on the three remaining MIGs.

MISSION 2—PHASE 3

⊕ **Situation:** The Scud C Tels have completed fueling and will launch within minutes. The enemy has been alerted and has reinforced the perimeter with armored personnel carriers.

⊕ **Mission:** Demolish the Scuds before they launch.

⊕ **Execution:** Destroy the armored personnel carriers. Demolish the Scuds by satchel charge. Radio HQ after you've done your job.

SQUAD SELECTION

Though this mission requires some heavy explosives, there are plenty of satchels scattered around the base camp for you to pick up. Select a mixture of heavy artillery (for use against the APCs) and a rifleman for best results in Mission 2—Phase 3. Outfit your squad as follows:

⊕ **Ranger One: Grenadier**—M16 with M203 grenade launcher, 2X scope, two satchels, two frag grenades, one smoke grenade.

⊕ **Ranger Two: Machine Gunner**—M249, two frag grenades, one medkit, one satchel.

TACTICAL PLAN

Begin this mission behind the safe cover of a truck. Don't rush out. Hidden enemies inhabit this small alcove and two nearby guard towers. Take the Machine Gunner and order the other Ranger to Hold Up. Cautiously move outside the cover of the truck. Rush to the first Scud missile launcher to the west. Take out the enemies behind the truck and in the guard tower. Place a satchel charge next to the base of the Scud missile and run back for cover behind the truck.

TIP There are two satchels, a medkit, and a flak vest to the southwest of the first Scud missile.

The satchel charge placed by the first Scud missile will likely take out both of them. If not, place a satchel charge by the second one, taking care to avoid enemy fire that may be coming from the guard tower to the north. Eradicate the remaining enemies from this area and head northwest along the road. You'll soon come face to face with the first armored personnel carrier. Stay out of its line of sight until you are ready to blow it to pieces.

The APCs pack a punch. If you stand in front of one for too long, it will be a matter of moments before you are pummeled with shells. There are a number of ways to destroy APCs. Here are a few:

⊕ **Placing satchels:** Although it's the riskiest method of removing the APCs, placing a satchel charge next to the personnel carriers

PART

III

will effectively remove them from existence. The hard part is getting close. The Ranger can only take a few shots from the APC cannon before biting the dust.

⊕ **Tossing grenades:** Hurling a frag or HE grenade at the APC will also destroy it. Use the posture keys to kneel, and then toss the grenade at the APC. Gauging distance can be tough, especially while you're being shot at. For added cover, toss a smoke grenade before you begin.

⊕ **Trusty grenade launcher:** The M203 grenade launcher is the easiest way to rid the world of the APC. One shot takes it out. Get close enough and let 'er rip (see Figure 8.3).

Figure 8.3

The APCs are tough, but not against the M203 grenade launcher.

After demolishing both APCs, you are free to charge into the final base camp. It's north of the last APC. Move far north into the canopy for cover. Pick up additional satchels and ammo inside. Take cover while maneuvering toward the Scud missile launchers. Place a satchel next to each Scud, and it will almost be time for the next mission. Radio HQ for extraction after destroying every Scud.

WARNING Enemies begin rushing from all sides after the last Scud missile is destroyed. Eliminate them before radioing HQ, or you could die before extraction.

MISSION 2—PHASE 3 DEBRIEFING

- Take out the enemies in the first alcove.

- Destroy the Scud missiles with satchel charges.

- Use the grenade launcher against the APCs.

- Take cover inside the canopy in the final alcove.

- Blow up the remaining Scud missiles with satchel charges.

- Eliminate your remaining enemies before radioing HQ.

MISSION 2—PHASE 4

⊕ **Situation:** USAF B2 bombers have air-launched their cruise missiles. They will impact in less than 15 minutes. *SOS Pavehawk* awaits to extract you when the mission's done. They're orbiting for exfiltration.

⊕ **Mission:** Destroy key targets in the chemical complex.

⊕ **Execution:** Demolish all pipe manifolds. Avoid poisonous gases. Destroy the remaining radar dish at the plant. Locate and board the helicopter for extraction.

SQUAD SELECTION

A Sniper is a must for this mission. The many enemies positioned around the pipe manifolds are easy targets for a Sniper equipped with a 4X scope. You need plenty of heavy explosives and you will find some during the mission. For good results, take this squad:

⊕ **Ranger One: Grenadier**—M16 with M203 grenade launcher, 2X scope, two satchels, two frag grenades.

⊕ **Ranger Two: Sniper**—SSG with 4X scope, one medkit, one satchel, one HE grenade.

PART

III

TACTICAL PLAN

Immediately switch Rangers and select your Sniper. The first two pipe manifolds are just north of your position. Carefully move forward until you spot the enemy guards patrolling the area or standing by the barracks. Use the Sniper's 4X scope to eliminate the four guards at the first manifold. Additional enemies will rush in from the forest. You'll want to take them out with a sniper rifle or M16.

Land mines line each pipe manifold. Be careful when approaching the manifolds and keep your Ranger far away by issuing the Hold Up command. Place a satchel charge next to the first pipe manifold and run for cover. You can also toss a HE grenade at the pipe manifold.

WARNING When you destroy a pipe manifold, you unleash poison gas onto the land. Don't stand too close to the exploding manifold, or you'll die from the fumes. Order your Ranger to Hold Up and keep him a safe distance from the gas.

The next pipe manifold is just north of this position. Keep your Sniper in the lead, sweep the area and eliminate enemies that emerge from the trees. A small camp will appear with enemy guards around the pipe manifold and near the barracks. Order your partner to Hold Up or Fire 'Em Up while you use the Sniper to remove all guards from the area. Destroy the pipe manifold with another satchel charge or HE grenade (see Figure 8.4). Head north through some hills and trees to reach the third pipe manifold.

Figure 8.4
Look out for that poisonous gas!

TIP Two satchel charges are to the east of the second pipe manifold. A medkit and flak vest are in the forest to the north of the second manifold.

A small camp appears after the forest. Again pick off enemy guards with a Sniper and 4X scope. Use your other Ranger, equipped with an M16 and grenade launcher, to clean up any additional enemies. Toss a HE grenade at the final pipe manifold (or place a satchel charge). Remember to keep away from the explosion, or poison gas will envelop you.

Head west toward the radar dome—your last target. Use the structures nearby for cover while one Ranger places a satchel charge next to the dome. Retreat from the dome quickly and call HQ for the extraction helicopter. Head south toward the landing zone. If you become lost while searching for the helicopter, remember you can use the GPS to learn its location. Board the helicopter and pat yourself on the back. This was a tough mission and you pulled it off.

MISSION 2—PHASE 4 DEBRIEFING

- Move north. Take out enemy guards with the Sniper's 4X scope.

- Destroy the first pipe manifold with a satchel charge or HE grenade. Avoid land mines and poison gas.

- Move north, taking out enemy guards.

- Blow up the second pipe manifold.

- Move through the forest to the third pipe manifold and destroy it.

- Head west to the radar dome. Take it out too.

- Radio HQ to send the helicopter.

- Move south using the GPS to locate your extraction helicopter.

PART

III

CHAPTER 9

Colombia—
The Magdalena River

While on patrol in the Gulf of Mexico, the *USS Lewis* captures a freighter holding 12 tons of cocaine. In retaliation, narcoterrorists ambush a U.S. Army convoy. The Chairman of the Joint Chiefs of Staff (CJCS) vows to continue counter narcotics operations. Satellite imaging locates the narcoterrorist training camp in the Magdalena River basin. A SOCF team discovers the narcoterrorist leader, Colonel Marcos, inside a well-guarded compound. A Ranger team approaches on riverine boats and attempts to infiltrate the compound and capture Marcos.

Once you've apprehended Colonel Marcos, Special Operations Command Headquarters (SOCOM HQ) orders the Ranger team to destroy the enemy barracks and drug labs with heavy explosives. After you wipe out the narcoterrorist base camp, escort Colonel Marcos to the extraction helicopter for delivery to the authorities.

MISSION 3—PHASE 1

⊕ **Situation:** Enemy forces are unaware of Ranger team infiltration. SOCOM intelligence indicates Colonel Marcos is in the compound with his bodyguards.

⊕ **Mission:** Locate and capture Colonel Marcos.

⊕ **Execution:** Find Colonel Marcos and his bodyguards. Kill the bodyguards but don't injure Colonel Marcos. Do not allow him to evade capture either. Radio SOCOM HQ when you've completed the mission.

SQUAD SELECTION

Although this mission is fairly short, visibility is a constant problem. The Amazon jungle is murky and dark. A steady rain makes it even more difficult to see what lies ahead. For this phase, select a Sniper to pick off narcoterrorists in the guard tower and a Close Quarters Ranger to eliminate enemies who sneak up or hide behind trees. Outfit your squad as follows:

⊕ **Ranger One: Sniper**—SSG with 4✕ scope, one medkit, one satchel, one NV scope, two frag grenades.

⊕ **Ranger Two: Close Quarters**—I-37 (Ithaca 37), two medkits, one satchel, one frag grenade, one extra clip.

TACTICAL PLAN

Begin this mission on a dock just off the river. Rain is constant, and visibility is especially tough. Switch on your GPS and head south. Keep your Sniper in front ,and use the 4✕ scope or NV scope and SSG to knock off guards as you approach the southern camp. You will arrive at a small shack with a guard inside. Remove him with the Sniper. This area is a dead end, but an extra medkit and flak vest are behind the shack.

PART

III

Head back north toward your start position and pick up the road moving due north. Order your partner to Follow Me. Follow the dirt road into the jungle. You should have no trouble reaching Colonel Marcos as long as you keep the road in sight. The road never heads west. If your GPS reports you are on a west heading for any extended period, it's the wrong way. When all else fails, your GPS indicator glows green in the direction you should be heading. Let the GPS guide you back to the road.

Don't use the road. Narcoterrorists have placed land mines all along the road. Follow alongside on the grass to the left or right of the road.

The trickiest segment in this phase is finding narcoterrorists hidden behind foliage and trees. Most remain well hidden until you are nearly on top of them. The Sniper won't help you much here. Deep in the jungle, you need the Close Quarters Ranger in the lead position. He carries the powerful Ithaca. At close range, it is a devastating weapon. You can take out these cowards before they get off a shot.

As you follow the road, you'll eventually come to a guard tower holding an irritated narcoterrorist. Use the Sniper to empty the guard tower from a safe distance. Continue toward the enemy camp. Follow the road through two forks—stay left the first time, and then hang a right at the second fork.

 TIP Although you don't have to investigate enemy structures inside this base, a flak vest and medkit are on the second floor.

Colonel Marcos looms at road's end. You'll know him by his white suit and hat (see Figure 9.1). He will express his displeasure about the prospect of being captured by shooting at you. To capture Marcos, charge him and he'll surrender by throwing his arms in the air. Be fast because he'll likely be firing at you and you can't take too much damage. If you miss, he'll flee into the enemy base. Follow him inside and capture him. The mission automatically ends when you have captured the narcoterrorist leader.

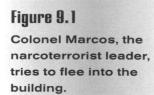

Figure 9.1
Colonel Marcos, the narcoterrorist leader, tries to flee into the building.

WARNING Bodyguards might surround Colonel Marcos. Pick off his henchmen from a distance with the Sniper—but don't shoot Colonel Marcos! If you accidentally kill him, the mission ends in failure.

MISSION 3—PHASE 1 DEBRIEFING

- Move south from the start position to collect an extra medkit and a flak vest.

- Follow the winding road through the jungle.

- Beware of land mines placed in the middle of the road.

- Use your Sniper against narcoterrorists in the guard tower.

- After entering the base, find Colonel Marcos. He's positioned to the far southwest and wears a white suit and hat.

- Don't kill Marcos or the mission fails. Run into Marcos to capture him.

PART

III

MISSION 3—PHASE 2

⊕ **Situation:** Enemy forces remain in the narcoterrorist training camp. Marcos' men remain unaware of the Ranger presence in the area.

⊕ **Mission:** Raid the training camp and destroy key targets.

⊕ **Execution:** Find the enemy camp and penetrate their defenses. Demolish all barracks and stockpiles by satchel charge. Destroy all remaining enemy forces in the camp. Radio SOCOM HQ when the mission is done.

SQUAD SELECTION

To complete this mission, you need to equip yourself with at least five heavy explosives. Enemies positioned in high guard towers and inside protective bunkers are another problem. Take a Grenadier for the extra grenade firepower and a Sniper with 4X scope to dispose of the guards. Outfit your squad as follows:

⊕ **Ranger One: Grenadier**—M16 with M203 grenade launcher, 2X scope, one medkit, two satchels.

⊕ **Ranger Two: Sniper**—SSG with 4X scope, one medkit, one satchel, two frag grenades, one HE grenade.

TACTICAL PLAN

This second phase of Mission 3 mirrors the first. Visibility is a continuing problem, with dense, murky jungle and steady sheets of rain. Getting lost isn't an issue since you are constrained to a simple dirt road. Switch on your GPS and head north. If you get turned around or even lost, check your GPS—the glowing direction indicator will guide the way. For now, put your Sniper in the lead position. Enemy troops are hiding behind trees and in bunkers. Move cautiously with your hand ready on the 4X scope.

The road bends to the east with a guard tower shrouded in jungle foliage to the west. Use your Sniper to pick off the guard from a distance. Continue following the road as it winds north and east, finally coming to a rickety wooden bridge. Cross the bridge heading east.

WARNING Land mines cover the dirt road. Farther along, land mines are placed outside the road as well. Move with caution at all times. Be aware of your partner behind you.

Soon after the bridge you cross the bridge, you'll see a bunker to the left of the road. These enemies are tough to hit unless you use your Sniper and 4X scope. Position yourself between trees to the left of the road and take them out. The road curves to the southeast and into the enemy training camp. Continue to watch for land mines, both on and off the road, and for enemies hiding behind trees and foliage.

The camp entrance is ahead. The camp is in a big alcove surrounded by impenetrable forest. Inside the camp are five barracks and a couple of guard towers with sniper guards. Narcoterrorist training equipment litters the area, making for excellent cover if needed (see Figure 9.2). Select the Sniper and take out any guards you can scope from a distance, particularly in the guard towers. Move into the camp. Conceal yourself behind the training equipment as you clear the area and prepare to destroy the barracks.

Figure 9.2:
Use the training grounds for cover.

PART

III

TIP Before demolishing the five barracks, scamper inside each to capture goodies such as HE grenades, machine gun ammo, satchels, and medkits.

Use Ranger orders extensively inside the camp. Switch to the Grenadier and fire the M203 grenade launcher at the barracks to destroy them. Give the Sniper the Fire 'Em Up or Hold Up command so he'll cover you. The satchels will destroy buildings, but the grenade launcher is much faster. After you've destroyed the barracks and cleared the camp of enemies, radio SOCOM HQ for your next mission.

MISSION 3—PHASE 2 DEBRIEFING

- Head north, looking out for the guard tower on the west side of the road.

- Proceed with caution since the road is scattered with land mines.

- After the wooden bridge, use a Sniper and 4X scope on the two narcoterrorists huddled in the bunker to the left of the road.

- Use the Sniper to remove the guards from the base towers.

- Collect extra ammo, satchels, and HE grenades before blowing up the barracks.

- Use the Grenadier and M203 grenade launcher to destroy the five barracks. Satchel charges could help too.

MISSION 3—PHASE 3

⊕ **Situation:** Recon has detected the center of Colonel Marcos' drug operations. Enemy forces are unaware of Ranger team infiltration.

⊕ **Mission:** Raid the coca camp and call in a close air strike.

⊕ **Execution:** Recon the camp and eliminate enemy guards. Call in a close air strike with a smoke grenade. Locate and board the helicopter for extraction.

SQUAD SELECTION

Mission briefing says you need a smoke grenade to call in the air strike but don't outfit your squad with one. You will come upon a smoke grenade during the mission.
Do remember to take a Sniper. Guards fill the jungle and most are well protected by
foliage and bunkers. Select a Close Quarters Ranger to join the Sniper. His Ithaca
will come in handy during close jungle combat. Outfit your squad as follows:

⊕ **Ranger One: Sniper**—SSG with 4X scope, two medkits, one
  satchel.

⊕ **Ranger Two: Close Quarters**—I-37 (Ithaca 37), two medkits,
  one satchel, one frag grenade, one extra clip.

TACTICAL PLAN

Perhaps the most difficult mission, the last phase of Mission 3 requires several tactics
for your survival. Begin inside the coca camp. Select the Sniper, switch on the GPS,
and move to the west, following the dirt path. Stay covered in the trees to avoid land
mines near the buildings. Turn right and take out the guard near the first drug lab.
Move forward, eliminating the guards ahead of you in the foliage and beside the
other structures. Be sure to check behind. A few enemies will sneak up on you. Order
your partner to Hold Up or Fire 'Em Up to cover your back.

After clearing the area, move to the center of camp and toss the smoke grenade.
Don't call in the air strike until you have followed the road out of camp. Once you
and your partner are clear, call in the air strike on your SATCOM radio.

TIP Don't check every drug lab for enemies. Your objective is to clear
enough foes to safely toss the smoke grenade and radio in the air strike.
Drug lab occupants won't make it through the fiery explosions.

When the camp is destroyed, you'll receive a message from HQ that Colonel
Marcos has escaped. You have new orders: kill him on sight. Follow the road deeper
into the jungle. Marcos rests at the end of the winding road. As you exit the coca
camp, there's a guard tower on your right. Use the Sniper to eliminate the guard.

PART

III

The road features the occasional land mine. Most enemies hide among the trees and foliage. If you remain on the road, you will be caught in a crossfire. Move through the trees on the left side of the road. Use the Close Quarters Ranger to terminate narcoterrorists along the path.

Two bunkers and an abandoned house filled with opponents will give you the most trouble. Both bunkers, as well as the house, contain enemies. Terrorists camped across the road from the bunkers will tear you up if you ignore them. Order the Close Quarters Ranger to Hold Up and use the Sniper exclusively. Stay in the prone posture. You will be harder to hit, and the SSG (see Figure 9.3) will still be accurate. There's plenty of cover here. After eliminating enemies from the bunker and house, use the structures to your advantage.

Figure 9.3

Get low against enemies who are protected by bunkers.

TIP Clearing bunkers of narcoterrorists is tough. Crouch as you approach the bunker, and shoot a sniper rifle. Then toss a grenade.

Colonel Marcos is in a large clearing and he's wearing a white suit and hat. Unlike other narcoterrorists, Marcos can withstand some shots before finally going down. Use the Close Quarters Ranger, armed with the Ithaca, to take him out. Use the prone position to make yourself harder to hit. Once Marcos is dead, radio HQ to call in the extraction chopper. Use your GPS to locate the landing zone in this alcove.

MISSION 3—PHASE 3 DEBRIEFING

- Clear the immediate area—the drug lab camp—of foes with your Sniper.

- Throw a smoke grenade at the center of the drug labs.

- Follow the road out of the drug lab camp and radio in the air strike.

- Don't always use the road. Move among the trees where enemies hide.

- Be careful near enemy bunkers. Use a Sniper or grenades to remove guards from their posts.

- Marcos requires several shots. Use your Close Quarters Ranger to take him out. Stay in the prone posture to avoid taking too many hits.

- Radio HQ to call in the helicopter. Use the GPS to locate the landing zone.

PART

III

CHAPTER 10

Honduras–
Sierra de Soconusco

The USASOC (Special Operations Command) Nuclear Crisis Team responds to a break-in by a heavily armed paramilitary unit. A group calling themselves the Omega Militia seized 2 kg of weapons-grade plutonium in the break-in. To complicate matters, the Omega Militia also has a trigger device with the potential to detonate a nuclear weapon. Two cellular phone transmissions from the Omega commander are intercepted and traced to the Sierra de Soconusco mountain range in Honduras. Satellite reconnaissance locates vehicles that make up the Omega's mobile command post. A Ranger team is sent to recover the plutonium and avert a nuclear disaster. Additional mission objectives include apprehension and interrogation of an Omega Militia member and disruption of a news broadcast televising a speech by an Omega subcommander.

MISSION 4—PHASE 1

⊕ **Situation:** The enemy is on a high state of alert. Militia commanders are inside the perimeter.

⊕ **Mission:** Penetrate militia defenses and demolish the perimeter gate.

⊕ **Execution:** Recon the militia perimeter. Clear the area of enemy forces. Assault and demolish the main gate by satchel charge. Radio SOCOM HQ when the mission is complete.

SQUAD SELECTION

The path to the perimeter gate is cluttered with bunkers and guard towers. You'll need a Sniper to catch the enemies off guard. The Grenadier is especially helpful because of the effectiveness of his M203 grenade launcher. Annihilate the bunker by firing a grenade inside it. Outfit your squad as follows:

⊕ **Ranger One: Sniper**—BMP50 with 4X scope, one medkit, one satchel, one HE grenade.

⊕ **Ranger Two: Grenadier**—M16 with M203 grenade launcher, two medkits, one satchel.

TACTICAL PLAN

Begin this mission on a gravel road at the top of a mountain. The road winds down the mountain and curves north and south as it descends. The perimeter gate rests at the bottom of the mountain. Choose the Sniper initially and pick off nearby guards. Switch on your GPS and head northwest. Far ahead, you will see the first of many bunkers. Fire your sniper rifle at the guard inside. Collect the M203 rounds inside with your Grenadier. Follow the curving road southeast and use the same technique on the bunker to the right.

TIP To destroy the second bunker, head to the first barrel at the right of the road. Select the Grenadier and peer over the cliff to the northeast. Use the ACOG scope and aim your M203 inside the bunker. Fire now and watch the pyrotechnics.

After the second bunker, you will arrive at a parked bus. Use the vacant vehicle for cover against enemies in the third bunker ahead and to the left. Move ahead between the parked bus and junked car (there is a land mine to the right—be careful). Search the third bunker for extra ammo and a medkit. Follow the road east and use the Sniper against the guard tower ahead. The road bends northward. Pick off the tower guards with the Sniper. Inside there's another medkit.

WARNING Be careful traversing this winding road. Enemies are armed with M203 grenade launchers. If you stand still, they will get a fix on you and lob a grenade your way.

Continue down the road slowly. Use the Sniper to shoot the guards in the tower ahead at the curve. After the curve, the last stretch of road leads to some barbed wire barricades. Use the Sniper to pick off guards patrolling the barricade. They are atop the perimeter gate or in nearby bunkers.

After the area is clear of foes, take out the gate. Move around the barbed wire barricade to the left, and approach. Fire a grenade at the gate with your Grenadier—one will do the trick (see Figure 10.1). If the grenade isn't your style, you can plant a satchel charge at the gate's base and watch the explosion. Call HQ on the radio and prepare for the next mission.

Figure 10.1
Take out the perimeter gate with a well-placed grenade.

MISSION 4—PHASE 1 DEBRIEFING

- Have the Sniper clear the start position of enemy guards.

- At the first barrel, use the Grenadier to peer over the cliff and fire a grenade at the bunker to the east.

- Fire the Sniper to wipe out guards protected by towers and bunkers.

- Collect medkits from the vacated bunkers.

- Don't stand still too long; some enemies have M203 grenade launchers.

- Pick off guards at the gate and the barricade with the Sniper.

- Fire a grenade at the gate or use a satchel charge to destroy it.

MISSION 4—PHASE 2

Situation: A TV news crew is preparing to transmit a speech by the militia subcommander. The broadcast could cause widespread public panic and must be prevented.

Mission: Infiltrate the base, demolish communications, and capture the militia officer.

Execution: Penetrate enemy defenses, and then locate the TV news van. Demolish the news van's SATCOM dish before the broadcast. Capture the subcommander and interrogate him. Radio SOCOM HQ when the mission is finished.

SQUAD SELECTION

Once again, a Sniper in your two-man squad will fend off cleverly hidden guards. Many enemies in this phase are armed with grenade launchers, so you want to take them out as quickly as possible. The SATCOM dish needs to be destroyed from long range. A Grenadier would be a wise choice. Outfit your squad as follows:

⊕ **Ranger One: Sniper**—BMP 50 with 4X scope, three medkits, one HE grenade.

⊕ **Ranger Two: Grenadier**—M16 with M203 grenade launcher, 2X scope, four medkits, one FG grenade, one HE grenade.

TACTICAL PLAN

This mission begins at a dead-end road. Turn on your GPS and begin to head south. A few guards are up ahead on either side of the road. Move your Sniper forward and pick them off. Continue moving south as the road curves southeast and back south again through several parked trailers.

Use the trailers for cover. Enemies are camped behind each trailer and some charge from the western hills.

TIP Instead of confronting enemies hiding behind the trailers, shoot at their feet! Assume the prone posture with your Sniper and shoot their legs. A direct shot will put them on the ground and you can safely continue.

Follow the road, keeping an eye out for guards hiding inside foliage on either side of the road. Much like the last phase, many bad guys are armed with M203 grenade launchers. Don't stand still too long or you are bound to take a grenade to the face. Use the Sniper's 4X scope to quickly scan the area for well-hidden enemies, taking them out before they have a chance to fire off a grenade.

Eventually you will come to a metallic tanker station on the left side of the road. Two guards are high on the catwalk. Use the Sniper and scope to relieve them of their duty. Another guard is stationed under the tanker station. Take him out before moving in close. More guards will charge from the right side of the road after you have secured the station—kill them with your Sniper or Grenadier.

TIP After securing the station, order one Ranger to Hold Up. Use the other Ranger to investigate the top of the station, where there's an additional medkit.

Move east and then south past another set of parked vehicles. Use them for cover against enemy soldiers who inhabit the area. Again, be careful not to stand around too long. Enemies equipped with grenade launchers are excellent shots when you stand still. Past the vehicles, the terrain will slope upward and end at a small enemy camp containing the news van.

Enter the base by keeping left. A few guards stand near pipes and machinery. Terminate them with your Sniper, and then use the machinery as cover against other foot soldiers. A few structures with enemy patrols are across the base. Eliminate them with your Sniper's BMP50 (see Figure 10.2). Once the base is secure, you are free to destroy the news van.

Figure 10.2

With the crosshair positioned on target, pull the trigger.

Find the vehicle with the satellite dish on top—that's the news van. Select your Grenadier and stand back a good distance. Use your ACOG to get a precise aim and fire a grenade at the dish. When the dish is destroyed, the enemy subcommander will flee the van and attempt to escape, using the route by which you came. Intercept by running into him. The mission will end.

PART

III

WARNING Be prepared. After you destroy the SATCOM dish, the subcommander could flee the scene. You might have trouble catching him. If he escapes back to the start position, the mission ends in failure.

MISSION 4—PHASE 2 DEBRIEFING

- At the start position, a few enemies are hiding up the road among bushes. Use the Sniper as lead Ranger and take them out.

- When you reach the first batch of parked trailers, assume a prone position and put a bullet in the legs of an enemy.

- After killing the guards at the metallic tank structure, use one Ranger to climb to the top. A medkit will reward your efforts.

- At all times, keep an eye on the hills to each side of the road. Enemies are well hidden in the foliage.

- Keep left in the final base camp, taking out guards and using the machinery as cover.

- Use the Grenadier to fire a grenade at the SATCOM dish on the news van.

- Intercept the subcommander as he flees the van. If he gets away, the mission fails.

MISSION 4—PHASE 3

⊕ **Situation:** The militia commander has been alerted and is attempting to flee with the plutonium.

⊕ **Mission:** Use any force necessary to secure the plutonium.

Excuction: Destroy any enemy vehicles and guards. Assault the plutonium transfer point. Capture the militia commander and secure the plutonium. Locate and board the helicopter for extraction.

Squad Selection

To recover the plutonium case, you are required to assault a well-fortified enemy stronghold. Guards are scattered around the camp, many carrying M203 grenade launchers. Enemy firepower will come from all sides in this operation. Hordes of bad guys are high on catwalks and are protected by pillars and boxes. Select the Recon Ranger and equip him with the 4X scope for sniping and five medkits. Select the Grenadier for the battle against the militia commander. It's much easier with a grenade launcher. Outfit your Rangers as follows:

Ranger One: Grenadier—M16 with M203 grenade launcher, 2X scope, four medkits, two frag grenades.

Ranger Two: Recon—MP5, 4X scope, five medkits, two extra clips.

Tactical Plan

The enemy stronghold is to the west of the start position. Don't head directly to the base; enemy fire will overwhelm you. Instead, turn on your GPS and head southwest. From this point, use your Recon Ranger and the 4X scope to remove any guards patrolling the outer perimeter. Follow the cliff side around and head due west. Once the structure is in sight, turn north and take out the guards. Move under the structure to begin the heart of your operation.

Once you have reached the structure, pick up the road heading northeast underneath the enemy stronghold. You should see a parked truck up ahead. When you reach the truck, order your Recon Ranger to Hold Up by the truck. Then, order the Recon to Fire 'Em Up so he will defend himself. Select the Grenadier and follow the ramp up to the higher floors of the stronghold.

TIP Look closely around the truck. There's a medkit placed next to one of the tires.

Move to the top floor and head southwest down the tunnel. Head straight to the end and pick up the medkit and flak vest hidden here. Turn back around and move through the entry to your right. You are now on the roof of the stronghold where the militia commander is hiding the plutonium case. Use your M16 and 2× scope to remove the guards from the roof (see Figure 10.3).

Figure 10.3

After eliminating the guards, climb to the roof.

Make your way out onto the roof using boxes for cover. Two sets of boxes are in the center of the roof. The militia commander is hiding behind the box formation to the right. Switch to the M203 grenade launcher and fire a few grenades at the militia commander and the boxes. The dead commander will drop the plutonium case. Switch to your Recon Ranger.

The militia commander's death triggers more enemy guards who rush the stronghold. Use your Recon Ranger to terminate the guards who have arrived at the base and are on the ramp leading to the top floors. When the area is clear and a safe route secure, switch back to your Grenadier to begin your escape.

WARNING If your Recon Ranger is dead when you kill the militia commander, you'll have a difficult time escaping the stronghold. Try to keep the Recon Ranger alive by switching to him periodically during the mission to verify that his area is clear of enemies.

You should find the plutonium case where you killed the militia commander. Pick up the case and radio HQ for the extraction helicopter. Use your GPS to get the heading to the landing zone. If you used the Recon Ranger to secure an escape route, control the Grenadier down the ramps and onto the surface. If you run into additional enemies, use the Grenadier's M16 and 2X scope to eliminate them. Once you have reached the landing zone, board the helicopter to begin your next mission.

MISSION 4—PHASE 3 DEBRIEFING

- Don't head immediately toward the stronghold to the west. Instead, patrol the outer perimeter, heading southwest and eliminating all guards.

- After the perimeter is secure, head inside the stronghold and follow the road northeast.

- Use the ramp by the parked truck to gain access to higher floors.

- Collect the medkit and flak vest at the end of the tunnel.

- On the rooftop, use the Grenadier against the militia commander to retrieve the plutonium case.

- Radio in for extraction, using your GPS to find the landing zone.

PART

III

CHAPTER 11

Afghanistan— The City of Kabul

AUnited Nations special envoy and U.S. Senator Galore travel to Afghanistan for talks on establishing the city of Kabul as a UN safe haven. Mujahadeen rebels attack the diplomatic enclave and take the Senator hostage. The Mujahadeen rebels plan to execute Senator Galore if their demands are not met within 48 hours. Before the deadline, the President orders a rescue attempt. U.S. Marines evacuate other diplomats and their families from Kabul as a Ranger team is sent to infiltrate the rebel camp and rescue the Senator. An Afghani rocket launcher pointed at Fort Bala Hassir also threatens Senator Galore since that is her reported location. Your Ranger team is ordered to eliminate the rocket launcher before proceeding to Fort Bala Hassir.

MISSION 5—PHASE 1

⊕ **Situation:** Afghani forces feuding with the Mujahadeen have aimed a rocket launcher at Fort Bala Hassir. This poses an immediate threat to the Senator.

⊕ **Mission:** Find and destroy the rocket launcher.

⊕ **Execution:** Recon the city block. Clear enemy forces from the area. Destroy the rocket launcher. Radio SOCOM HQ when you've accomplished the mission.

SQUAD SELECTION

This mission is overflowing with enemy soldiers, some on foot scampering through the streets and others perched high in buildings using sniper rifles to pick you off. Select the Grenadier for his M16 assault rifle and grenade launcher to take care of the ground forces, and select the Sniper to exterminate the opposing sniper soldiers. Outfit your squad as follows:

⊕ **Ranger One: Grenadier**—M16 with M203 grenade launcher, 2X scope, three medkits, one satchel charge.

⊕ **Ranger Two: Sniper**—SSG with 4X scope, one NV scope, two medkits, one HE grenade, three frag grenades.

TACTICAL PLAN

This mission requires a trek through a city block that contains enemy soldiers at strategic positions. The city is large and you can venture off to explore if you want. However, your safest bet is to stick with the GPS direction indicator. Switch on the GPS and follow the glowing indicator to the rocket launcher.

TIP From your start position, turn south and head into the dead end. A medkit is behind the shack.

PART

III

Select the Grenadier and move forward. Up ahead you will see a fork in the road—keep to the left, taking the road to the northeast. Use the Grenadier's M16 and ACOG scope to remove enemies from the sides of the road. Since the mission is dark, use night vision goggles to get a good look at oncoming enemies. The 2X and 4X scopes will not be as useful as the ACOG or NV scope, because there's so little light.

WARNING Don't run in the middle of the road—snipers are everywhere. Hug the buildings and you'll be much more difficult to hit.

The road will bend to the east and you will see a tank up ahead. The tank is mobile so don't get too close. Use the Grenadier's M203 grenade launcher to take it out with one hit. After you pass the destroyed tank, turn north and run back into the alley—there's a flak vest behind the building (see Figure 11.1). Return to the road and head southeast, still following the road.

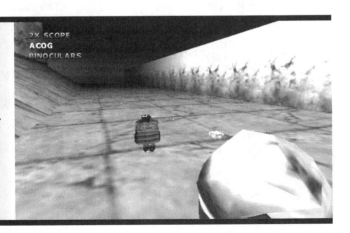

Figure 11.1

Pick up all the flak vests. You'll need as many as you can get.

Keep a good eye on your GPS. If you get lost or turned around, you can easily ascertain where the rocket launcher is stationed by looking for the glowing GPS indicator. The road will continue southeast, bending east and then making a sharp right to the south. Along the road, you'll want to switch between the Sniper and the Grenadier. Use the Sniper to eliminate enemies perched on rooftops and balconies and use the Grenadier against ground soldiers.

Take another sharp right, following the road to the west. Hug the buildings on the left. Between two buildings is an alley that contains another flak vest. Take it for more protection against enemy snipers. Many foot soldiers are in this area. Move to the right side of the road and use the debris as cover against many enemies. When the area is secure, continue moving west until you reach a fork in the road. Hang a right at the fork and continue east through city streets.

Turn left at the next intersection, moving south along the road. Up ahead is a bridge, which slopes downward and continues south to another intersection. Turn right and follow the road southwest. Eventually you will come to another turn. Follow the road to the east and then back to the north. Another flak vest is in an alley on the right side of the road. Pick it up and continue.

Enemy snipers and ground troops abound on this final stretch of road. The rocket launcher is ahead in an alcove (see Figure 11.2). You must secure the area before attempting to destroy the launcher. One shot from the snipers can mean certain death. Stay close to the building walls, and inch forward, picking off soldiers with your Sniper.

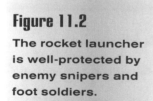

Figure 11.2

The rocket launcher is well-protected by enemy snipers and foot soldiers.

Once the alcove is secure, move in and destroy the rocket launcher with your grenade launcher or satchel charge. To complete the mission, radio HQ.

This mission is one of the most difficult in the game because of enemy snipers, who can remove you from the scene with a single shot. Take plenty of medkits with you and grab all the flak vests in the mission. Follow your GPS and hang close to the buildings. Move cautiously forward, using your scope extensively to scan for enemies.

PART
III

MISSION 5—PHASE 1 DEBRIEFING

- Switch on the GPS and follow its glowing directional indicator.

- Destroy the tank with your Grenadier's M203.

- Recover every flak vest on the way to the mission objective.

- Stay close to the buildings and away from the road's center.

- Don't explore—follow the path to the rocket launcher.

- Beware of enemy snipers perched on high balconies.

- Destroy the rocket launcher with an explosive.

MISSION 5—PHASE 2

Situation: The rebels are defending against air assault with 3 antiaircraft guns positioned on the fort's outer walls.

Mission: Infiltrate the fort and destroy all gun emplacements.

Execution: Demolish the entrance gate by satchel charge. Eliminate enemy personnel. Destroy all three antiaircraft guns. Radio SOCOM HQ when the mission is finished.

SQUAD SELECTION

This mission requires at least four heavy explosives—three to destroy the antiair gun placements and one to knock out the main gate. Choose the Grenadier to join your squad for his M16 and lightning-quick grenade launcher. Select the Rifleman for the ground warfare. Here's how to outfit your squad:

Ranger One: Rifleman—M4, 2✕ scope, three medkits, one satchel, two frag grenades.

Ranger Two: Grenadier—M16 with M203 grenade launcher, 2× scope, two medkits, one satchel.

TACTICAL PLAN

Begin this phase in front of the enemy base. The GPS is nonfunctional in this mission so you won't be able to get the coordinates for mission objectives. Two tents are nearby; turn to face the base, and head to the tent on the right where a few guards stand in front. Use your ACOG scope and assault rifle to remove them. Inside the tent you'll find extra ammo, a satchel charge, and a medkit.

When the base entrance is clear of enemy soldiers, approach the main gate. Beware of the barbwire barricade protecting the entrance. Land mines are strewn about, so don't get too close. The main gate can be destroyed by satchel charge, claymore, or grenade launcher. Fire the Grenadier's M203 at each door, and cautiously enter the base.

TIP Once you enter the base, use the debris inside for cover. Several armed guards are stationed in the initial courtyard. Crouch behind debris and eliminate them.

Two antiair guns are off to the right of the base entrance and one is positioned to the left. Climb the stairs to the left. Order your Rifleman to Fire 'Em Up and guard the stairs in case any soldiers decide to approach. The antiair gun is ahead. Select the satchel charge in your inventory and place the device next to the gun. Set the timer for 30 seconds and run down the stairs, ordering your Rifleman to follow.

WARNING After you destroy an antiair gun, more guards will rush out of the base. Take your time approaching the other antiair guns. Use your ACOG or 2× scope to pick off guards from a distance.

Climb up the right staircase now. The first antiair gun on this side is ahead. Place a satchel charge next to the gun, set the timer for 30 seconds, and retreat back down the staircase (see Figure 11.3). Once it's destroyed, go up the staircase and follow the path into another large courtyard.

PART

III

Figure 11.3

Use a satchel charge to destroy amtiair guns.

As you approach the final antiair gun, you will be on a high walkway looking out over a courtyard. Enemies fill the courtyard and they're protected behind debris and cement blocks. Move cautiously down this walkway. There's no protection here and you are vulnerable to enemy fire. Use the ACOG or 2X scope to terminate enemies below. Approach the final antiair gun and destroy it with a satchel charge. After all three antiair gun placements are out of commission, radio HQ to begin the next phase.

WARNING Be careful if you use the M203 grenade launcher when destroying antiair guns. The blast radius is huge. If your Grenadier is too close, he won't survive.

MISSION 5—PHASE 2 DEBRIEFING

- Search the right side tent for extra ammo, a satchel charge, and a medkit.

- Clear the area of guards. Stay away from barbed wires and mine fields.

- Use the Grenadier's M203 to destroy the front gate.

- From what was the front gate, three antiair gun placements are to the right and left of the stairs.

- Use satchel charges to destroy the antiair guns.

- Radio HQ once the mission is accomplished.

MISSION 5—PHASE 3

⊕ **Situation:** The deadline for the execution of the Senator has passed.

⊕ **Mission:** Rescue the Senator before she is executed. Safely exfiltrate the Senator. Get her out of there.

⊕ **Execution:** Recon the fort and find the Senator. Kill any rebel guards and rescue the Senator. Safely guide Senator Galore to the extraction point. Locate and board the helicopter for extraction.

SQUAD SELECTION

With a mixture of ground troops and snipers positioned at high posts, this phase definitely requires a Sniper Ranger. Many areas are lit, so the 4✕ scope will be especially useful. Also select the Recon Ranger to handle the ground forces with his MP5 and large stash of medkits. Outfit your squad as follows:

⊕ **Ranger One: Sniper**—SSG with 4✕ scope, four medkits, one frag grenade.

⊕ **Ranger Two: Recon**—MP5, 2✕ scope, five medkits, two extra clips.

TACTICAL PLAN

As in the previous phase, the GPS is nonfunctional. You must search the fort to locate the Senator. From the start position, head through the alley until you come to a right turn. Keep the Sniper in the lead. Many guards in the first few areas are atop high walkways.

Move forward through the alley and keep to the left. The path forks up ahead. The right path leads into a large courtyard. The left path leads directly to the Senator.

TIP If you venture into the courtyard, hug the right wall. Take the staircase leading to the walkway and turn right to a dead end, where there's an extra medkit, a flak vest, and several boxes of ammunition.

Take the left path until you can turn left. Head into the tunnel. Have your Recon Ranger eliminate any ground soldiers hiding inside the tunnel. When you have exited the short tunnel, go left and follow the path. This area is filled with blocks and debris and several enemies camped about. Use the debris to your advantage by crouching or using the prone posture to protect yourself. Toss some frag grenades or use your scopes to exterminate all foes. Move on once the enemy guards have been terminated.

You will come to a right turn. Turn right and follow the path to the end. Turn left and approach the final area with extreme caution. A Mujahadeen rebel is preparing to execute the Senator. If he sees you, he will terminate her immediately. Select the Sniper Ranger and use the 4✕ scope. Strafe to the side slowly until you capture the guard in its crosshairs (see Figure 11.4). Take out the guard and move forward. To rescue the Senator, touch her.

After the Senator is rescued, she grabs the guard's AK47 to arm herself. Radio HQ to call in the extraction helicopter and retrace your steps. The landing zone is in the large courtyard just before the short tunnel you passed through.

WARNING Don't let the Senator venture in front of your Rangers. You don't want to shoot her accidentally. She can withstand only one bullet. If the Senator is killed, the phase ends in failure.

Figure 11.4

Don't let this guard see you, or he'll terminate Senator Galore.

Keeping the Senator alive until you reach the extraction helicopter can be this mission's most difficult challenge. Here are two strategies to keep Senator Galore alive:

 Order the Senator to Hold Up: After you rescue Senator Galore, order her to Hold Up. Use your Recon Ranger to clear a path to the landing zone. After the area is secure, move back and escort the Senator to the helicopter.

 Order the Senator to Follow Me: Select one of your Rangers and have Senator Galore follow to the landing zone. This is the most difficult option. It's difficult to keep track of enemy guards coming up from behind, and the Senator can occasionally wander into crossfire. If the Senator takes a bullet, the phase ends in failure.

MISSION 5—PHASE 3 DEBRIEFING

- Use the Sniper as lead Ranger to eliminate guards from high posts.

- Out in the courtyard, follow the stairs on the left to retrieve extra ammo, a flak vest, and a medkit.

- Take cover behind blocks and debris.

- Move slowly when approaching the Senator and use your Sniper's 4X scope to take out the guard who is preparing to execute her.

- Radio HQ to send the extraction helicopter.

- Escort the Senator to the landing zone by clearing a rescue route with one of your Rangers.

- Move out to the courtyard to reach the helicopter.

PART

III

CHAPTER 12

Pale, Bosnia—1998

Amber Star—an operations cell of the North Atlantic Treaty Organization (NATO)— approved the arrest of Bosnian war criminals. The Secretary of Defense (SECDEF) and Chairman of the Joint Chiefs of Staff (CJCS) select General Ratko Mladic, Commander of the Bosnian Serb army, as the first target. Mladic is captured and detained at the Implementation Force (IFOR) airbase in Tulza. Soon, Radovan Karadzic orders a mortar attack against the IFOR airbase. Satellite Communications (SATCOM) intercepts a cell call from Karadzic and triangulates his location. Special Operations Command (SOCOM) orders a Ranger team to capture Karadzic. SOCOM wants intelligence about enemy positions. Your job is to seize the forward op (the forward objective point where intelligence on enemy positions is stored) and raid a nearby Serbian militia base. The plan is to get Karadzic.

MISSION 6—PHASE 1

⊕ **Situation:** Serbian militia forces control the mountain base. The forward op possesses intelligence on enemy positions.

⊕ **Mission:** Raid the Serbian base.

⊕ **Execution:** Seize the forward op and raid the Serbian militia base. Secure intel and report to SOCOM. Radio SOCOM HQ when the mission is done.

SQUAD SELECTION

This mission requires both the brute force of the Grenadier and the finesse of the Sniper. Enemies are everywhere and they are vigilant in protecting their two bases, the forward op and the militia base. You must overpower them. Outfit your **Ranger** team as follows:

⊕ **Ranger One: Sniper**—SSG with 4X scope, three medkits, two frag grenades, one HE grenade.

⊕ **Ranger Two: Grenadier**—M16 with M203 grenade launcher, four medkits, one HE grenade, one WP grenade.

TACTICAL PLAN

Advance with extreme caution. It's tough sighting enemy troops because the forest and hills obscure them. There are two goals. The first is to seize a small stronghold and recover intel—the map that reveals enemy positions. The second is to secure and defend the Serbian militia base until reinforcements arrive.

You can attack the forward op from the front or rear. Here's how:

⊕ **Front assault:** If you attack the forward op from the front, you'll need to face south at the start position and move through a dangerous valley. Enemy snipers are on either side ready to pounce on anyone who wanders into sight. Use your Sniper to clear out everyone you see. When the area is clear, select the Grenadier and climb the hill to the left. Order your Sniper Ranger to Hold

PART

III

Up. Take out enemy snipers sitting here at close range with the M16 (unless you already wasted them with the Sniper).

When all is clear, select the Sniper and follow the Grenadier up the hill. From this hill, use the Sniper to eliminate guards on the opposite hill and in front of the forward op, which is to the south. Advance cautiously into the forward op, taking note of mines strewn around the perimeter. Use the building and surrounding debris as cover until you eliminate all enemies.

 Rear assault: Instead of turning south and entering the valley, follow the road east. Eliminate the enemies on the road and also those perched in the hills to the right. Continue to advance until you come to an opening on the left side of the road heading west. Inside this opening, you'll see a disabled enemy vehicle. From this point, head up the hill to the left facing north.

To take the hill, scale the snow bank—not the rocky terrain. The easiest access is on the far right of the hill. Continue north and you'll reach the southern side of the forward op (see Figure 12.1). Use your Sniper to eliminate guards positioned behind debris. Take cover and eliminate the Serbian troops.

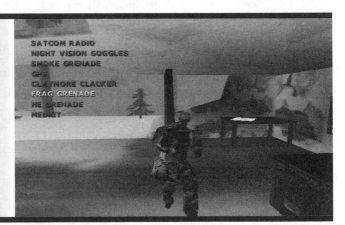

Figure 12.1

Your first mission objective is to seize the forward op where intelligence on enemy positions is stored.

Once the area is clear, move inside the structure and search to the left of the two green boxes. The enemy map—the intel you're after—is on the desk. Approach the map, grab it, and report to HQ. Head south out of the forward op.

Follow the snowy hill down until you reach what's left of an enemy vehicle. Face west to spot the road, and follow the road south until you reach an enemy minefield. Use the Sniper against enemy soldiers positioned high on the hills on either side of the road.

TIP Just before the minefield, climb up the hill to the right of the road. A few enemy snipers defend the hill, where there's a flak vest.

At the land mines, turn north and climb the hill and spot the fence up ahead. At the fence, turn north and follow until you see an opening into the militia base on your left. Some troops may be positioned at the fence. Use your Grenadier's M203, and fire grenades at their feet. Enter the base, being careful not to trip the land mine at the entrance, and approach the first house, moving south past it to a second house. At this point, SOCOM HQ will notify you that reinforcements are on the way—just hold the militia base for five minutes (see Figure 12.2).

Figure 12.2

Hold the militia base for five minutes until reinforcements arrive.

TIP Investigate the first house after entering the base. Under the ramp that leads to the balcony, you'll find some HE grenades. On the balcony, there's an extra medkit.

Enemy soldiers will rush the base from all sides. Use the structures as cover, and watch your back and your partner's back against enemies assaulting from the rear. If you have been recovering weapons from dead soldiers, your Sniper should be equipped with an assault rifle. Use it to defend the base. Also, you can use the Grenadier to fire grenades at the fence, which is protecting advancing enemies. Beware of troops on the roofs. Hold the base for five minutes until reinforcements arrive. Once the timer expires, this phase will conclude.

TIP Position the Grenadier on the balcony of the first house, and then order the Grenadier to Fire 'Em Up. He'll protect that side of the base from enemy attempts to go inside.

MISSION 6—PHASE 1 DEBRIEFING

- Head to the forward op and assault it from the front or rear.

- Use your Grenadier to eliminate ground troops at close range. Use your Sniper to pick off enemies high on hills and behind trees.

- Secure the forward op by using the structure as cover, terminating advancing foes. Grab the intel on the desk next to the boxes.

- Move south out of the forward op and pick up the road to the west.

- Follow the road until land mines impede your progress.

- Turn north and move into the Serbian militia Base.

- Hold the base for five minutes until reinforcements arrive.

MISSION 6—PHASE 2

⊕ **Situation:** The Serbian commander has been located. Serbian militia presence in the area is heavy.

⊕ **Mission:** Capture the Serbian war criminal.

⊕ **Execution:** Clear the buildings for use as a base of operations. Secure the checkpoint along the road. Capture the Serbian commander alive. Radio SOCOM HQ when you've accomplished the mission.

SQUAD SELECTION

Serbian troops are everywhere in this mission and are particularly well-protected inside the structures. Select a Sniper Ranger to terminate foes from a distance, and use the Recon Ranger to clear out the structures. Outfit your Ranger team as follows:

⊕ **Ranger One: Sniper**—SSG with 4X scope, four medkits, one frag grenade.

⊕ **Ranger Two: Recon**—HK G11, 4X scope, two extra clips, four medkits, two frag grenades, one HE grenade.

TACTICAL PLAN

Although HQ orders you to clear the buildings, the real mission objective is to capture the Serbian commander, Radovan Karadzic alive. Much like the previous phase, multiple paths can lead to a successful conclusion.

Your first objective is to find the road and follow it into the Serbian camp, where the commander is preparing to leave in a truck. There are multiple ways to reach the road—all filled with equal danger. Before you head out, grab the HE grenades near the start position.

⊕ **East from start position:** Turn on your GPS and head east. Use your Sniper to pick off enemy soldiers waiting for you behind trees in this short valley. The path also contains land mines, which need to be avoided or shot. Order your Recon

PART

III

Ranger to Follow Me and pick up the road just up ahead. Follow the road north, and when it forks, keep to the right. This road leads east through a covered bridge to the Serbian commander.

North from start position: Switch on your GPS and head north, taking out enemy patrols with your Sniper. Watch the hill to the north; some troops are stationed here. Move northeast until you see the road. Follow the road east to reach the Serbian commander.

Southeast from start position: Turn on your GPS and head southeast. A set of buildings filled with Serbian troops is ahead. Use your Sniper as lead Ranger and the 4X scope to eliminate the soldiers. Spot the road just northeast of the houses and follow. At the fork, keep left, head northwest and follow the road to the Serbian commander.

TIP Eliminating enemy troops from protective structures is difficult. Use your Sniper to take them out. Order the Recon Ranger to Fire 'Em Up so he'll watch your back. Use every means of protection—use the crouch and prone posture and take cover behind trees and debris. Toss grenades into the structures.

At the road, follow north and east through a covered bridge. Take out the guards protecting the bridge with your Recon Ranger and continue heading south. A small set of structures is on the right of the road. Enemies are everywhere. If you decide to ignore them and continue, they will chase you. Take out as many Serbs as possible with your Sniper. If you enter the structures, beware of the land mine protecting the entrance and use your Recon Ranger to attack camping enemies at close range (see Figure 12.3).

Follow the road south until you reach a truck. As you approach, the truck will begin moving and head in your direction. HQ will radio that Radovan Karadzic is on the truck. Karadzic must be taken alive, so you have no choice but to follow the truck. Retrace your steps along the road.

Follow the road north, through the covered bridge and then south. The road will fork. Keep to the left and continue pursuing the truck northeast. The truck will come to a stop inside an enemy camp.

Figure 12.3
Use the Recon Ranger to terminate the remaining enemies hiding inside the structure.

TIP At the fork in the road, there's a demolished enemy vehicle. Search the vehicle for a flak vest.

Commander Karadzic stands to the left of the parked truck—identify him by his red cap (the other soldiers are wearing green). Another Serbian base camp is on the left side of the road. Some troops may rush out of the structures to aid Karadzic. Have your Sniper eliminate any troops from the structures' perimeter.

To capture Karadzic, just charge him. He'll be shooting at you, so move with caution. Order your partner to Hold Up or you risk Karadzic being killed by your partner's itchy trigger finger. The mission concludes when the Serbian Commander is apprehended alive.

MISSION 6—PHASE 2 DEBRIEFING

- Reach the road by heading north, east, or southeast from the start position.

- Move north and east along the road, eliminating guards in the area and at the covered bridge.

- Remove the Serbian troops from the structures on the side of the road.

PART

III

(Continued on next page)

(Continued from previous page)

- **Approach the truck. Karadzic will attempt a getaway.**

- **Follow the truck into the Serbian base.**

- **Capture Karadzic by charging him. Do not kill him.**

MISSION 6—PHASE 3

⊕ **Situation:** A United Nations Outpost has been overrun by Serbian forces. The base is vital to UN peacekeeping operations. Hostile reinforcements are expected.

⊕ **Mission:** Secure the UN base.

⊕ **Execution:** Seize control of the base from the Serbian militia. Defend the base from counterattack. Radio SOCOM when the mission has been accomplished.

SQUAD SELECTION

The Grenadier is a wise choice for this mission because of the destructive power of his M203 grenade launcher and his lightning quick M16. Also select the Recon Ranger with a 4× scope, for the ability to carry plenty of ammo and eliminate guards from a distance. Be sure to take along a satchel charge to destroy a bridge late in the mission. Outfit your Ranger squad as follows:

⊕ **Ranger One: Recon**—MP5, 4× scope, three medkits, one satchel, two extra clips.

⊕ **Ranger Two: Grenadier**—M16 with M203 grenade launcher, 2× scope, four medkits, one frag grenade, two WP grenades.

TACTICAL PLAN

Switch on your GPS, and then head southeast and approach the small outpost. Serbian forces, stationed by the wooden fence, are patrolling the outer perimeter. Shooting them with your Recon Ranger will be tough; use the Grenadier to fire grenades over the fence and at their feet. Once the outpost is secure, continue moving southeast into another set of three structures—this is the UN outpost.

On the approach, tap your Recon Ranger to take out any Serbs who are visible. One of the structures features a ramp leading to the roof. Clear out the forces and climb the ramp. Use your Recon Ranger from this vantage point to clear out any remaining troops from the surrounding grounds.

TIP Check under the ramp that leads to the roof. A flak vest is stashed underneath.

Once you've secured the UN outpost, enemy Serbs will begin rushing from all sides. SOCOM HQ will radio in, alerting you to defend the base from counterattack. Use the structures to your advantage and let the enemy come to you. Use the Recon Ranger's scope to eliminate foes from a distance. After the base is secure, SOCOM HQ will radio a report of an enemy installation north of your position. Check that your GPS is on, and follow the road north. Enemy Serbs are patrolling the hills to the side of the road; eliminate them with your Recon Ranger. Move through the installation gate and over a bridge to reach the enemy headquarters.

WARNING Enemy Serbs have placed land mines around their installation's gate—be careful when approaching, and snipe them from a distance.

Move inside the installation. Terminate the Serbian stationed in the guard tower. The Serbian supplies are located underneath a canopy. Pick up the flak vest inside the canopy, and then switch to the Grenadier and fire a grenade at the Serbian supplies. Once the supplies have been destroyed, SOCOM HQ orders you to blow up the bridge south of the installation. Head out of the installation, picking off Serbian stragglers as you go.

When you reach the bridge, place a satchel charge in the center, set the timer for 30 seconds, and continue following the road south. When the bridge is destroyed,

PART

III

SOCOM HQ will radio in again, announcing the extraction helicopter has been deployed. Check your GPS, and follow the indicator toward the landing zone (see Figure 12.4).

Figure 12.4

Exit the enemy installation, blow up the bridge, and head for the helicopter.

On your way to the landing zone, you'll reach several damaged structures. Enemies are hiding within and will chase you to the helicopter if you don't eliminate them. Use the Grenadier to lob some grenades into the structure and the Recon Ranger to terminate them from the road. Follow the road to the east.

At road's end, turn left and head north and you'll see the extraction helicopter. Board the helicopter quickly to complete the mission.

MISSION 6—PHASE 3 DEBRIEFING

- Turn on your GPS and head southeast into the first small outpost.

- Use the Grenadier to terminate enemies positioned behind the wooden fence.

- Once the first outpost is clear, move southeast to the UN outpost.

- Defend the UN outpost. Use the buildings as cover and let the enemy approach you.

- Follow the road northeast. Take the left fork and head north.

- Enter the enemy installation and eliminate Serbian forces inside, destroying their supplies under the canopy.

- Move south and blow up the bridge with a satchel charge.

- Use your GPS and follow the indicator to the landing zone.

- Board the extraction helicopter at the end of the road.

PART

III

CHAPTER 13

Thon an Thai, Vietnam—1969

When the North Vietnamese Army (NVA) launched the Tet Offensive, the 1st Brigade was involved in another campaign—called Operation Jeb Stuart. A B-52 supporting this campaign refueled while en route to North Vietnam on a mission to destroy an NVA supply depot. North Vietnamese air support shot down the B-52 before it completed its mission. B-52 Pilot F. Efigenio survived and parachuted into the 1st Brigade's area of operations. SOCOM HQ ordered the Long Range Reconnaissance Patrol (LRRP) to launch a search-and-rescue mission for the downed pilot. Meanwhile, a Ranger team attacks heavy-weapon platoons in Thon an Thai, while the 1st Brigade heads north to connect with the Ranger team.

MISSION 7—PHASE 1

⊕ **Situation:** The 1st Brigade is moving from the south. NVA operations are based east of Quang Tri. NVA weapon caches are hidden in nearby villages.

⊕ **Mission:** Disrupt NVA operations.

⊕ **Execution:** Find all weapon crates and demolish them. Ambush NVA forces. Clear the area of enemy forces. Radio SOCOM HQ when you've accomplished the mission.

SQUAD SELECTION

Your tour of duty in Vietnam is unique in that the selection of firearms is limited. Many weapons in *Spec Ops* were developed after the Vietnam War. You won't have access to powerful weapons such as the M203 grenade launcher, M4, MP5 and HK G11. Here are the weapons available for Rangers in Vietnam:

⊕ **M16**

⊕ **Ithaca 37**

⊕ **SSG (2✕ scope, 4✕ scope)**

⊕ **M60**

Since there's no M203 grenade launcher, equip your Rangers with at least three heavy explosives to destroy the weapon crates. North Vietnamese troops amass in the jungle. To eliminate many enemy troops, select the Machine Gunner and Rifleman since they come with plenty of ammo. Outfit your Rangers as follows:

⊕ **Ranger One: Machine Gunner—**M60, two medkits, one satchel.

⊕ **Ranger Two: Rifleman—**M16, 4✕ scope, three medkits, two claymores, two frag grenades.

169

TACTICAL PLAN

The location of the three weapon crates differs each time you begin this phase. In each instance, the crates are inside three North Vietnamese villages at fixed locations on the map. Begin the phase facing an intersection, with paths leading northeast, northwest, and south deeper into the jungle. Each path leads your Ranger squad into a village. Choose the northeast route to reach the closest North Vietnamese village.

While there are three villages in this mission, each village could hold one or more weapon crates. The number of crates in each village changes each time you restart. Your goal, then, is to visit each village to be sure you haven't missed any weapon crates. The GPS (or compass, as it's called in Vietnam missions) provides direction. Switch the compass on and keep it active for the entire phase. The glowing indicator will guide you to all targets in each village.

From the start position, follow the path northeast. North Vietnamese troops crowd all paths. Avoid enemy fire by hiding behind trees and foliage; crouch and lie prone to avoid enemy fire. Continue advancing northeast until you reach another intersection, with paths leading northeast, southwest, and west.

WARNING Approach all intersections with caution. The NVA has placed land mines at the center of each intersection. Destroy the mines from a distance with a scope. Get too close, and you'll need a medic or a coroner.

Keep following the path northeast to reach the first of the three villages. Thatch huts are inside the clearing. Weapon crates might or might not be inside this village. Look under each hut for the blue crates that hold the weapon stashes. Take cover in the huts and eliminate any troops in the area. Order your Ranger partner to Hold Up and set a claymore or satchel charge next to the crates. Go into the village when the crates are destroyed.

TIP Search the village huts for additional ammo and a satchel charge. Be aware the North Vietnamese have mined the ramps leading to the huts.

After you have explored the first village, head west into another jungle path. Move with caution as the paths are usually filled with adversaries. Use the Rifleman's

4X scope to scan long range for enemy soldiers. After a short trek west, you'll arrive at the second village.

Search the village once again for weapon crates. Destroy any crates you see beneath the huts with a satchel charge or claymore mine, and then take the path west out of the second village (see Figure 13.1).

Figure 13.1

The crates are no match for your claymore mines.

Follow the path west as it curves southwest and finally south. North Vietnamese soldiers camp along the path, hiding behind trees and in small hills. Move forward cautiously. You'll come to a large clearing where cover is minimal—hide behind each tree. Many troops patrol this clearing. Take out the troops from a distance with your scope, and then move behind the next tree and fire again.

Continue south through the clearing, but take special care to scan the ground for land mines with your scopes. The field is heavily mined. Cross the bridge. The last village is ahead.

TIP HE grenades, ammo, and a flak vest lie inside huts in the third village.

As before, search below the huts for blue crates. If you find any, set a satchel charge or claymore mine next to them. The phase ends automatically when you destroy all three weapon crates.

PART

III

MISSION 7 — PHASE 1 DEBRIEFING

- It's easy to get lost deep in the jungle. Switch on your compass. Follow the directional indicator to each village.

- Look out for land mines at intersections.

- Take cover behind trees and structures.

- Search village huts for weapon crates.

- Use satchel charges or claymore mines to destroy weapon crates.

- Collect HE grenades, satchels, and a flak vest from the village huts.

MISSION 7—PHASE 2

⊕ **Situation:** NVA heavy-weapon platoons control the area of operations. The 1st Brigade is attacking in support of the LRRP operation.

⊕ **Mission:** Destroy the NVA's heavy-weapon platoons in Thon an Thai.

⊕ **Execution:** Recon and secure all areas around Thon an Thai. Destroy NVA emplacements and clear the area of enemy forces. Radio SOCOM HQ when the mission is successful.

SQUAD SELECTION

Equip your Ranger squad with plenty of heavy explosives. The NVA emplacements consist of six mortar launchers—all of which must be destroyed by heavy explosive.

The Rifleman is the best choice since he comes with the powerful (and ammo-rich) M16, 4× scope, and an ability to hold four heavy explosives. Outfit your squad as follows:

⊕ **Ranger One: Rifleman**—M16, 4× scope, three medkits, two claymores, two frag grenades.

⊕ **Ranger Two: Rifleman**—M16, 4× scope, three medkits, two claymores, two frag grenades.

TACTICAL PLAN

Switch on the compass at the start; turn around and face east. The small clearing ahead holds the first set of NVA emplacements. Approach, but don't enter the clearing. Stay out of range of enemy troops and select the 4× scope. Scan the clearing for North Vietnamese troops and eliminate them with your M16. Look for troops protected by the circular bunkers. Your mission is to destroy NVA mortar launchers inside those bunkers.

Once you've cleared the area of visible troops, move in cautiously, with your mouse hand ready to bring up the 4× scope. This clearing features the first set of mortar launchers you are to destroy. There are two more sets in the surrounding jungle.

WARNING Don't approach the circular bunkers without first eliminating the troops inside. Many troops inside the bunkers carry rocket launchers and some might even fire mortar launchers. You'll be dead, either way, if they get a shot off.

Move inside each circular bunker and place a claymore mine next to the mortar launcher (a frag grenade will also work). Retreat to a safe distance and use the claymore clacker to detonate the mine, destroying the mortar launcher. There's ample cover in these clearings. If any enemy troops are left, crouch behind the bunkers or other debris and take them out.

After you destroy both mortar launchers in this clearing, retrace your steps west and follow the curving path northwest until you reach the intersection. Beware the land mine at the center of the intersection. Head west and follow the jungle path northwest into another clearing.

TIP Much like the last phase, enemy troops hide along the jungle paths. Use the trees as cover and approach with caution. Use your Rifleman's 4X scope to get a good look at patrolling troops before they see you.

Don't move into the clearing until you have eliminated as many enemies as you can. Pay special attention to soldiers stationed inside the circular bunkers. Use the 4X scope to take them out. Once the clearing is secure, move into the circular bunkers and destroy the two mortar launchers. Use claymore mines or frag grenades to destroy the two NVA heavy weapons (see Figure 13.2). After both are destroyed, it's time to move to the final clearing and the last two mortar launchers.

Figure 13.2

Place a satchel charge or claymore mine next to the mortar launchers— then run like heck!

TIP Search the circular bunkers in the second clearing for a medkit, a satchel charge, and a flak vest.

From the second clearing head west into a winding jungle path. Trees will cover your from enemy troops. The path curves south and then southeast, leading to a junction where you can go southwest or northeast. Choose the southwest path into the final clearing.

Terminate North Vietnamese soldiers from long range with your M16 and 4X scope. When the area is secure, advance into the clearing and search the circular bunkers for the final set of mortar launchers. Place either a claymore mine or a frag grenade next to each mortar launcher to destroy them. When all six mortar launchers have been removed, the mission automatically ends.

TIP Search the circular bunkers in the third clearing for HE grenades and extra ammunition.

MISSION 7—PHASE 2 DEBRIEFING

- Switch on your compass. From the start position, head east.

- Use the 4× scope to eliminate guards from inside the bunkers.

- Destroy the two mortar launchers with heavy explosives.

- Head west and then northwest to reach the second set of NVA defenses.

- Eliminate the guards from the bunkers at long range.

- Destroy the two mortar launchers with heavy explosives.

- Collect a medkit, a satchel, and a flak vest from the enemy bunkers.

- Go west, and then follow the path south toward the final set of NVA emplacements.

- Eliminate the guards from the bunkers at long range.

- Destroy the two mortar launchers with heavy explosives.

PART

III

MISSION 7—PHASE 3

⊕ **Situation:** The B-52 pilot awaits pick up. Last known location is the crash site. HQ is unable to communicate with the pilot.

⊕ **Mission:** Rescue the B-52 bomber pilot.

⊕ **Execution:** Locate the downed aircraft. Search for survivors. Radio HQ when the mission is a success.

SQUAD SELECTION

This mission requires no heavy explosives—so stock up with medkits! Select the Rifleman and the Machine Gunner for their heavy firepower. Grab an extra clip for the Machine Gunner's M60. The enemy presence is heavy and escorting the downed pilot to the extraction helicopter will be especially tough without ample ammo. Outfit your Rangers as follows:

⊕ **Ranger One: Rifleman**—M16, 4✕ scope, five medkits, two frag grenades.

⊕ **Ranger Two: Machine Gunner**—M60, three medkits, one frag grenade, one extra clip.

TACTICAL PLAN

Switch on your compass and begin the mission at a four-way intersection. Instead of heading deep into the jungle (and probably getting lost) follow the path south to a small clearing. Several enemy troops inhabit the clearing but are particularly well hidden behind trees and foliage. Shoot the Rifleman's 4✕ scope to remove them at long range.

Head southwest into another jungle path filled with troops who are equally as likely to approach from the front as the rear. Watch your back, and move southwest along the path as it curves east. It leads into an enormous clearing filled with stone structures, ruins, and a large central temple.

WARNING Don't rush into the clearing. Enemy troops are everywhere, and cover is minimal until you reach the center. Use the 4× scope to take out all visible troops. Move in with caution.

Head east toward the large stone temple. As you approach the temple, alter your course northeast. The temple stands in the center of the clearing. There's plenty of cover here. Use debris and stone blocks as protection against North Vietnamese soldiers.

Follow the path out of the clearing to a downed aircraft in a small alcove. According to the mission briefing, this was the pilot's last known location. Search the aircraft; the pilot is no longer here (see Figure 13.3). Radio SOCOM HQ to confirm the pilot's missing status. HQ orders you to find him.

Figure 13.3

Approach the missing pilot's last known location, but watch out for nearby land mines placed by enemy troops.

Head southwest and retrace your steps back to the large clearing. The downed pilot is a prisoner on the second floor of the central stone temple. Steps on the east side of the temple lead to the second floor. Move up the stairs with one of your Rangers, and touch the pilot to free him.

With the pilot rescued, SOCOM HQ alerts you that the extraction helicopter has been deployed. Descend the temple steps and head southeast. The path leads outside the clearing where the helicopter awaits you. Board the helicopter to conclude the mission.

PART

III

WARNING Stay close to the pilot at all times. He is vulnerable to enemy fire. Clear yourself a path by scanning the area with your 4× scope. If the pilot is killed, the mission has failed.

MISSION 7 — PHASE 3 DEBRIEFING

- From the start position, head south into a clearing.

- Cover yourself against enemies in foliage and behind trees.

- Move southwest and follow the path into a large clearing.

- Go toward the left side of the temple and head northeast.

- Approach the crash site to receive the message from HQ ordering you to locate the missing pilot.

- Return to the large temple and use the steps to climb to the second floor. Locate and touch the captive pilot.

- From the temple, head southwest to locate the extraction helicopter. Escort the pilot to the helicopter and protect him from enemy troops.

CHAPTER 14

Rayat, Iraq—1996

The Secretary of Defense (SECDEF) and the Kuwaiti Defense Minister plan a secret raid to locate and destroy biological weapons. Their plan includes sending U.S. Air Force F-117 stealth fighters, which fly slower than the speed of sound and attack at night, to attack suspected Iraqi biological weapon bunkers. Battle damage assessment intelligence reveals the Iraqis have relocated the weapons. Headquarters then sends F-18 Navy fighter jets to attack potential storage locations. The bombing attacks strike a secret biological weapons storage bunker. National Security Agency satellites detect a new weapons assembly complex. HQ orders a Ranger team to infiltrate the Iraqi camp and destroy suspected chemical weapon sites. The mission objective includes escorting a supply truck filled with captured Iraqi weapons to a pickup site.

MISSION 8—PHASE 1

⊕ **Situation:** Iraqi forces are transferring biological weapons. Time on target is critical. They must be prevented from dispersing their deadly weapons.

⊕ **Mission:** Demolish Iraqi bio weapons.

⊕ **Execution:** Attack the bases before weapons transfer is complete. Clear the area of enemy forces. Avoid contamination by demolished weapons. Radio SOCOM HQ when the mission is complete.

SQUAD SELECTION

Don't begin this phase without a Grenadier on your Ranger squad. The Grenadier's M203 grenade launcher can be used to destroy the Iraqi biological weapon stores from a distance, which is easier and safer than placing satchels or tossing grenades. Also select the Rifleman to assist. His M4 and scope will come in handy against ground opposition. You could also select the Sniper, but his lack of ammo could make the mission difficult. Outfit your squad as follows:

⊕ **Ranger One: Grenadier—**M16 with M203 grenade launcher, 2✕ scope, three medkits, one satchel.

⊕ **Ranger Two: Rifleman—**M4, 2✕ scope, three medkits, one satchel, two frag grenades.

TACTICAL PLAN

Begin this phase between two mountains. Head either north or south. Both paths lead to the road you need, but the southern path puts you closer to the first of five batches of chemical storage units you must destroy to complete the mission. Timing is critical—you only have three minutes on the timer. As you complicate the Iraqi plans, the timer will increase with each site you destroy. Get on the road and head due west. Some Iraqi troops will be hiding in the trees to the left of the road and atop the hill to the right of the road. Use your Rifleman's M4 and scope to eliminate them.

Look out for Iraqi troops firing grenade launchers from guard towers. Continue until you reach a series of camouflaged bunkers. The bunker on the far left holds a stash of chemical weapons.

WARNING Don't take cover behind green barrels strewn about this operation. Toxic fluid fills the barrels and will unleash poison gas if the barrels are destroyed.

Take out the Iraqis at the three bunkers. Have the Rifleman remove the guard from the tower to the southwest of the bunkers. Use the Grenadier and his M203 grenade launcher to destroy chemical weapons in the leftmost bunker. You can also use a satchel charge to demolish the Iraqi storage unit. Order the Rifleman to Fire 'Em Up while you use the Grenadier to demolish the chemical weapons—he'll watch your back and protect you from enemy troops. One down, four to go.

Resume your course on the road, heading north through more barrels and Iraqi forces. Traveling the road, you are highly vulnerable to Iraqi soldiers perched on the hills to the left and right. Move forward cautiously, using your scope to pinpoint any hidden troops. Continue north until you reach a set of three structures housing more chemical weapons.

TIP A few land mines protect nearly every stash of chemical weapons. If you run out of explosives, use a scope to destroy the mine next to the chemical weapons. When the land mine detonates, it will demolish the chemicals.

Use the structures as cover against any Iraqi guards. Some guards perch on rooftops. Your scopes will take them out. There is a high tower to the northwest of the camp with an Iraqi Grenadier stationed on top. Take him out with your Rifleman. Be careful if you decide to climb the tower since there is a land mine protecting the stairs. Once you've eliminated the troops, use the Grenadier against the boxes of chemical weapons. Order your Rifleman to Hold Up so he'll stay back. After you've destroyed the boxes, poisonous gas fills the air. Don't get too close or you'll die instantly from the fumes (see Figure 14.1). After destroying all three structures, go back to the road and head east.

Continue east along the road until you come to the final chemical weapons complex. There's plenty of cover in this area. Use it to take out the remaining Iraqi soldiers near the storage facility. Once the area is secure, use the Grenadier to destroy the last boxes of chemical weapons. All five chemical weapon complexes are history. To complete the phase, radio SOCOM HQ and prepare for the next operation.

Figure 14.1
Beware of the poisonous gas after destroying the boxes of chemical weapons.

MISSION 8—PHASE 1 DEBRIEFING

- From the start position, head south. Use the Rifleman against Iraqi troops hiding behind trees on the right and on the hill across the road.

- Travel west until you reach a series of three bunkers.

- Destroy the leftmost bunker with the Grenadier's M203 or satchel charge.

- Continue north on the road until you reach three structures containing chemical weapons.

- Destroy the weapon stores with the grenade launcher or satchels.

- Follow the road east until you reach the final structure housing chemical weapons.

- Blow up the chemical weapons with the grenade launcher or a satchel charge. Radio SOCOM HQ to complete the phase.

PART

III

MISSION 8—PHASE 2

⊕ **Situation:** Captured biological weapons must be transported to a pickup site for analysis. Iraqi troops are deployed to stop the transport.

⊕ **Mission:** Deliver bio weapons to the exfiltration site.

⊕ **Execution:** Escort and defend the truck's cargo. Counterattack Iraqi ambushes. Radio SOCOM HQ when you've completed the mission.

SQUAD SELECTION

This escort mission requires you to stay close to the truck at all times, fending off Iraqi ambushes. Select the Sniper so he can pick off enemy troops camping behind trees and barrels. The Sniper can also destroy land mines along the road. Select the Recon—with his speedy MP5—and the 2✕ scope. Then you can snipe soldiers and land mines. Outfit your Rangers as follows:

⊕ **Ranger One: Recon**—MP5, 2✕ scope, four medkits, two frag grenades, one WP grenade, two extra clips.

⊕ **Ranger Two: Sniper**—SSG with 4✕ scope, four medkits, one frag grenade.

TACTICAL PLAN

From the start position, head southeast. Up ahead you will spot the supply depot and the truck. Order your Sniper or Recon Ranger to eliminate Iraqi soldiers hiding inside the complex. Use the Sniper to take out the Iraqi Grenadier inside the guard tower on the left. Again, beware of toxic barrels. They emit poison gas when destroyed.

The road to the pickup site is full of land mines. If the truck drives over a land mine, the cargo could explode and the mission will end in failure. The truck will only move ahead if you are beside it. You can move ahead, take care of the land mines and soldiers, and then come back for the truck. Leaving the truck unguarded is risky, and you have only so much time to complete the mission.

It's best to start the truck moving, advance and clear the area ahead of land mines and troops, and then return immediately to the truck. Don't let the truck out of your sight for too long. Keep a lookout behind and order one of your Rangers to Hold Up next to the stopped truck. Most of all, don't rush. There is plenty of time to complete the mission. If you rush the truck, it is likely to be destroyed by an Iraqi Grenadier or a mine.

After the complex has been cleared of troops, stand by the truck to start it moving. Select the Recon or Sniper so you can use the scope to take out any Iraqi troops you see ahead. Stay a little ahead of the truck. Scan the upcoming sides of the road for enemies.

TIP If you are overwhelmed by enemy troops, lag behind the truck so it will stop. Take time eliminating the Iraqi forces, keeping them far away from the truck. Once the area is clear, continue escorting the truck down the road.

The road will curve twice, first heading northwest and then heading back southeast. Continue to move ahead of the truck, sniping the land mines with either your Sniper or Recon Ranger. Clear the sides of the road with either Ranger. Your biggest problem will be Iraqi Grenadiers positioned behind land formations and in guard towers. Be sure to search all along the sides of the road and eliminate all troops from your path. Missed troops might try to attack the truck from the rear. Escort the truck down the bumpy road as it heads south into the pickup site (see Figure 14.2).

Figure 14.2
Keep close to the truck, scanning ahead for Iraqi troops.

WARNING While you should stay near the truck, don't stick *too* close. You'll want to stay about a half-truck's length in front. Your Rangers are fast enough to outpace the truck and stop it. If you're too close and see a land mine ahead, you may not be able to stop the truck.

As the truck approaches the base, the heart of the operation begins. As the truck turns a corner, heading southeast, move up ahead and take out troops around the perimeter of the pickup site. Iraqi forces have also placed three land mines at the pickup site entrance. Use your scopes to destroy the mines. Several structures are in the camp, including a guard tower and a few tents. Clear the base or risk having the truck destroyed. Some of the Iraqi soldiers are carrying grenade launchers and will be gunning for the truck.

TIP Search the base for extra supplies, including ammo, HE grenades, a medkit, and a flak vest.

Order your Sniper to Hold Up near the truck. Make sure the truck has stopped its movement into the base before proceeding. Next, move into the base and use the Recon Ranger's MP5 and scope to remove any Iraqi soldiers stationed on top of the tents.

Once the base is secure, head back to the truck and escort it into the base. The truck will park and the mission will conclude.

MISSION 8—PHASE 2 DEBRIEFING

- Travel southeast along the road until you reach the parked truck, next to the chemical storage station.

- Take out the guards at the storage station and in the guard tower.

- Escort the truck through the winding road. Move ahead of the truck, clearing the path of land mines and troops. Then return to the truck and continue escorting it.

- When the truck reaches the base, use scopes to remove Iraqi troops from high positions. Some troops are carrying grenade launchers that could destroy the truck.

- Search the small base for a medkit and a flak vest.

- Radio SOCOM HQ after the base is secure.

MISSION 8—PHASE 3

⊕ **Situation:** Interrogation of enemy POWs has revealed the existence of a secret storage bunker. SOCOM HQ believes the bunker contains VX-precursor chemicals.

⊕ **Mission:** Locate and demolish the secret bunker.

⊕ **Execution:** Recon and identify the Iraqi commander. Track the commander to the bunker without being detected. Radio SOCOM HQ when you've finished the mission.

SQUAD SELECTION

Take a satchel charge and a claymore mine on this final mission. After locating the secret bunker, HQ will order you to destroy the bio-weapon-precursor chemicals inside. Select the Recon Ranger and the Rifleman. You'll face plenty of opposition as you invade the camp on foot and will need a large supply of ammo. Outfit your squad as follows:

⊕ **Ranger One: Recon**—HK G11, 2✕ scope, four medkits, one satchel charge, one frag grenade.

⊕ **Ranger Two: Rifleman**—M4, 4✕ scope, four medkits, two frag grenades, one claymore.

TACTICAL PLAN

From the start position, head toward the guard tower. Iraqi enemies will use trees for cover all throughout this final phase. Move down the hill with caution, using your scopes and assault rifles to eliminate the troops. Eventually you will end your descent down the hill and come to a road. A guard tower and pipe station are across the road. Eliminate the guards.

 TIP After removing the guards from the pipe station, grab the medkit by one of the green pipes.

While facing the pipe station, turn right and follow the road. Several Iraqi soldiers will greet you as you travel the gravel path. Your biggest worries are Iraqi troops carrying grenade launchers. Scope ahead with your Recon or Rifleman. Keep an eye out for enemies hiding behind trees and corners.

 TIP If you feel vulnerable on the road, stay among the trees that cover either side of the road. They provide ample cover from Iraqi troops.

Eventually you will arrive at an Iraqi camp. Advance slowly and take out the troops by the tents and guard tower. Hug the mountain on your right; the secret bunker is inside the mountain. Enter the bunker, and HQ will order you by radio to destroy the bio-weapon-precursor chemicals. Place a satchel charge next to the crates inside the secret bunker (see Figure 14.3). Set the timer for 30 and make your escape.

Here's the tricky part: when you exit the bunker, move through the door opposite the one you came in through. Once the satchel has detonated, poison gas will fill the bunker and it will be impossible to move through. The extraction helicopter is opposite where you entered the bunker. After the crates blow apart, SOCOM HQ will send the helicopter to the landing zone. If you exit the way you came in, you'll be too far from the landing zone. A long trek means facing countless Iraqi soldiers annoyed that you destroyed their secret bunker.

So, head out the bunker from the opposite entrance. Move forward and enter the other Iraqi base. Eliminate any guards, and turn right and advance to find the road. The landing zone and helicopter are to the right of the road. Board the helicopter. You have completed your tour of duty!

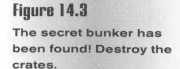

Figure 14.3

The secret bunker has been found! Destroy the crates.

MISSION 8—PHASE 3 DEBRIEFING

- From the start position, head straight toward the guard tower.

- Pick up a medkit by the pipe station across the road.

- Facing the pipe station, turn right and proceed down the road.

- Use trees and hills for cover.

- When you reach the Iraqi camp, turn right and hug the mountain.

- Enter the secret bunker. Destroy the crates.

- Exit the bunker from the other side and turn right until you reach the road.

- Turn left to locate the landing zone and extraction helicopter.

PART

III

APPENDIX A

Spec Ops
Scoring System

When a *Spec Ops* mission ends, the award screen appears. A series of rankings explain how well you did and what medals you could win for your efforts. This appendix explains how scores are evaluated and describes the medals.

AWARD SCREEN

The award screen appears after a mission ends, no matter whether you succeeded or failed in your duty. The screen information presents an overview of your performance in these categories (see Figure A.1):

Figure A.1

A successful mission will lead to honor.

- ⊕ **Enemies KIA:** How many enemies you killed.

- ⊕ **Rangers KIA:** How many Rangers you lost.

- ⊕ **Marksmanship:** How sharp was your accuracy in relation to the number of rounds fired.

- ⊕ **Completion Time:** How quickly you accomplished the mission.

- ⊕ **Mission Rating:** Overall rating based on the factors above.

- ⊕ **Best Rating:** Your best rating compared with previous attempts.

To achieve the highest possible score, you should complete each mission quickly and without taking casualties. Wipe out every enemy with accurate shots and don't fire wildly. If you do this—no easy task by any stretch—you'll be rewarded with a high score. Maybe even the Congressional Medal of Honor.

MEDALS

The medals in *Spec Ops* are based on real-world medals. As in real life, the U.S. government does not hand out these medals and awards to just anyone. Courage and selflessness count. Respect is earned. Earn respect in this game by mastering mission objectives, being quick, avoiding casualties, and conserving as much precious ammo as possible.

THE ARMY ACHIEVEMENT MEDAL

The Army Achievement Medal (AAM) was established by the Secretary of the Army on April 10, 1981. The AAM is awarded to any member of the Armed Forces of the United States, or to any member of the Armed Forces of a friendly foreign nation, who while serving in any capacity with the Army in a noncombat area distinguished himself or herself by meritorious service or achievement of a lesser degree than required for award of the Army Commendation Medal.

THE ARMY COMMENDATION MEDAL

The Army Commendation Medal (ARCOM) was established by War Department Circular 377 on December 18, 1945 (amended in DA General Orders 10 on March 31, 1960). The ARCOM is awarded to any member of the Armed Forces of the United States who while serving in any capacity with the Army after December 6, 1941, distinguishes himself or herself by heroism, meritorious achievement, or meritorious service. Award may be made to a member of the Armed Forces of a friendly foreign nation who after June 1, 1962, distinguished himself or herself by an act of heroism, extraordinary achievement, or meritorious service that has been of mutual benefit to a friendly nation and the United States. Awards of the ARCOM may be made for acts of valor performed under circumstances described above that are of lesser degree than required for award of the Bronze Star. These acts may involve aerial flight.

THE MERITORIOUS SERVICE MEDAL

The Meritorious Service Medal was established by Executive Order 11448 on January 16, 1969, as amended by Executive Order 12312 on July 2, 1981. The Meritorious Service Medal is awarded to any member of the Armed Forces of the United States, or to any member of the Armed Forces of a friendly foreign nation, who while serving in a non-combat area after January 16, 1969, distinguished himself or herself by outstanding meritorious achievement or service.

THE BRONZE STAR

The Bronze Star was established by Executive Order 9419 on February 4, 1944 (superseded by Executive Order 11046 on August 24, 1962). The Bronze Star is awarded to any person who while serving in any capacity in or with the Army of the United States after December 6, 1941, distinguished himself or herself by heroic or meritorious achievement or service, not involving participation in aerial flight, in connection with military operations against an armed enemy or while engaged in military operations involving conflict with an opposing armed force in which the United States is not a belligerent party. Awards may be made for acts of heroism, performed under circumstances described above, that are of lesser degree than required for the award of the Silver Star.

THE SILVER STAR

The Silver Star, section 3746, title 10, United States Code (10 USC 3746), was established by Act of Congress on July 9, 1918 (amended by act of July 25, 1963). The Silver Star is awarded to a person who, while serving in any capacity with the U.S. Army, is cited for gallantry in action against an enemy of the United States while engaged in military operations involving conflict with an opposing foreign force, or while serving with friendly foreign forces engaged in armed conflict against an opposing armed force in which the United States is not a belligerent party. The required gallantry, while of a lesser degree than that required for the Distinguished Service Cross, must nevertheless have been performed with marked distinction.

THE DISTINGUISHED SERVICE CROSS

The Distinguished Service Cross, section 3742, title 10, United States Code (10 USC 3742), was established by Act of Congress on July 9, 1918 (amended by act of July 25, 1963). The Distinguished Service Cross is awarded to a person who while serving in any capacity with the Army distinguished himself or herself by extraordinary heroism not justifying the award of a Medal of Honor, while engaged in an action against an enemy of the United States, while engaged in military operations involving conflict with an opposing or foreign force, or while serving with friendly foreign forces engaged in an armed conflict against an opposing armed force in which the United States is not a belligerent party. The act or acts of heroism must have been so notable and have involved risk of life so extraordinary as to set the individual apart from his or her comrades.

THE CONGRESSIONAL MEDAL OF HONOR

The Congressional Medal of Honor is the highest medal awarded by the United States. It has only been awarded 3,428 times in the nation's history. The Medal of Honor, section 3741, title 10, United States Code (10 USC 3741), was established by Joint Resolution of Congress on July 12, 1862 (amended by acts on July 9, 1918 and July 25, 1963). The Congressional Medal of Honor is awarded by the President in the name of Congress to a person who while a member of the Army distinguishes himself or herself conspicuously by gallantry and intrepidity at the risk of his life or her life above and beyond the call of duty, while engaged in an action against an enemy of the United States, while engaged in military operations involving conflict with an opposing foreign force, or while serving with friendly foreign forces engaged in an armed conflict against an opposing armed force in which the United States is not a belligerent party. The deed performed must have been one of personal bravery or self-sacrifice so conspicuous as to clearly distinguish the individual above his or her comrades and must have involved risk of life. Incontestable proof of the performance of the service will be exacted and each recommendation for the award of this decoration will be considered on the standard of extraordinary merit.

APPENDIX B

Internet Resources

The Internet has become the largest and fastest reference tool anywhere. With the click of a mouse button, you can find what you want if you know where to look. This list will steer you toward *Spec Ops* material, both real and fictional, and to modifications to alter your *Spec Ops* experience.

WEB SITES

Fortunately, there are plenty of resources around the Internet for *Spec Ops* players. You'll catch up with fellow players and multiplayer opponents on some sites, and you can discover user-created maps and modifications at others.

If you are new to the World Wide Web, here are the basics.

You need a modem for your computer (56K baud or faster preferred). You need an Internet service provider (ISP) to access the Internet. You need a browser to visit Web addresses. The two most popular browsers are Microsoft Internet Explorer and Netscape Navigator.

For info on our publisher's line of books and computer and video game strategy guides, visit:

http://www.sybex.com

For your convenience, this section is separated into discussions of three types of Web sites: *Spec Ops* fan sites, *Spec Ops* official sites, and reference addresses devoted to U.S. Special Forces.

SPEC OPS FAN SITES

A fan site is a Web page created by a game fan. Fan-site authors are loyal to the game and update their sites with new information when they can. Fan sites are not affiliated with Ripcord, the game distributor, or Zombie, the *Spec Ops* game designer, so some information at fan sites could be misleading.

WARNING Web sites—especially fan sites—are moving targets. Don't be surprised if some sites mentioned here suddenly disappear.

DELTA COMPANY

http://www.geocities.com/TimesSquare/Bunker/6116/

This fan site invites you to join their online squad and test your skills against other squads. With the new, multiplayer feature in *Spec Ops*, you can bet there will be tons of new squads forming all over the world.

Delta Company presents a roster of current members, including e-mail addresses, handles, rankings, and a simple application to join their ranks. *Delta Company* offers three live discussion forums, one for general comments about the game, one for platoon management, and a third for setting up matches with rival squads.

DEVIL'S BRIGADE

http://members.xoom.com/RipFire/spec.htm

Devil's Brigade is one more squad in the making for eager Internet players. Currently divided into three platoons, the *Devil's Brigade* actively recruits new members to play.

RANGERS ONLINE HANDBOOK

http://jeff.intraed.com/specops.asp

The *Rangers Online Handbook* presents updated *Spec Ops* news regularly and includes a fan forum to exchange ideas with other game fans. You can pick up game patches and modifications here too.

The *Rangers Online Handbook* is a valuable reference for mastering the unofficial *Spec Ops Scripting Language*, a program to radically alter the game's look and feel. You'll also come across tutorials and an array of modifications created by game fans.

SPEC OPS HOMEPAGE

http://www.1918.com/specops/home.html

This fan site is known for its detailed information on *Spec Ops* weapons and their real-world counterparts. The web site is also a gateway to connect to other sites of special interest to *Spec Ops* fans—without having to type in the other addresses.

SPEC OPS TACTICAL OPERATION COMMAND

http://specops.nobrainer.net

The *Spec Ops Tactical Operation Command* (SOTOC) offers readers news about *Spec Ops* modifications and Zombie's sequel, *Spec Ops 2*. Downloads, such as patches and the Voodoo 2 texture patch, are accessible through a bottom menu bar.

SOTOC is the source for the latest news and downloads. There are no mission hints or tips here, and data on user-created *Spec Ops* modifications is thin. Be forewarned: the author employs colorful language.

SPEC OPS SUPPLY DEPOT

http://home.bip.net/lowspirit/specops/

The *Spec Ops Supply Depot* supplies unique backgrounds, wav files, and icons for the Windows 95 operating system. A variety of styles and new material is uploaded frequently.

If you're a hard-core *Spec Ops* player, you owe it to yourself to check out free stuff you can download from the *Supply Depot*.

SPEC OPS OFFICIAL SITES

Official sites house the most accurate information, usually supplied by game programmers and designers. You'll find the latest official patches, demos, and information about sequels and other products in development.

RIPCORD GAMES

http://www.ripcordgames.com/games/specops/index.html

Ripcord is the official distributor of *Spec Ops*; its Web address is the only spot for technical support for game issues and for adapting to particular sound or video cards (see Figure B.1).

Figure B.1

Ripcord Games' official *Spec Ops* page

Beyond the official patches for *Spec Ops*, which you can obtain at Ripcord, there's a game demo where anyone can play and develop a feel for the game.

ZOMBIE'S SPEC OPS HOMEPAGE

http://www.zombie.com

While fan sites are usually on the ball when it comes to the latest news about *Spec Ops: Rangers Lead the Way*, the most reliable source is Zombie's official Web site (see Figure B.2).

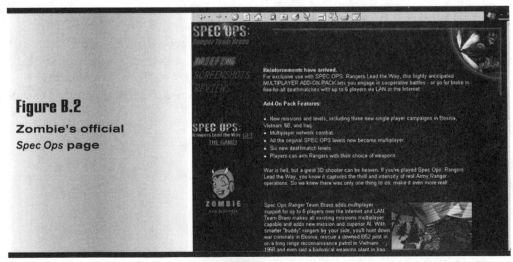

Figure B.2

Zombie's official *Spec Ops* page

These pages are updated regularly and the folks at Zombie have shown a high-level of commitment to *Spec Ops* by releasing patches to fix control configuration and to improve artificial intelligence. For Voodoo 2 owners, Zombie released a batch of high-resolution textures so owners of the powerful 3DFXcard can get more from their game.

REFERENCE SITES

The game *Spec Ops* no doubt made you curious about real-world Special Forces. A wealth of information is just a mouse click away. Here are a few select Web sites.

NIGHT STALKERS

http://www.nightstalkers.com/

Night Stalkers is a resource for Ranger information, supplying articles, historical essays, a Hall of Honor, poems, prayers, and creeds.

You'll find a considerable amount of information pertaining to the heritage of the Special Forces, infamous members throughout time, what it's like to train and recruit for the Special Forces, and a gift shop with memorabilia.

SPECIAL OPERATIONS

http://specialoperations.com/

This is the motherlode of Special Forces information with a library on every Special Forces operation launched by the U.S. government, and lists and descriptions of every weapon and piece of equipment actively used by the Special Forces.

There's a humor section, information on memorial sites, special activities open to the public, resources for veterans, and links to hundreds of military organizations.

THE DROP ZONE

http://www.thedropzone.org/new.html

The *Drop Zone* is a fantastic online museum catering to all things Special Forces. Most content is by members of the Special Forces reflecting on missions where they participated. Sometimes humorous, often chilling, the *Drop Zone* gives perspective on *Spec Ops* like no other Internet site.

The *Drop Zone* is easy to navigate, with articles organized by subject and theater. You will encounter intense, historical memories and leave with a renewed respect and understanding of just what it means to be a Ranger.

MODIFICATIONS

Modifications, or mods, are small files to alter some part of your gaming experience. Neither Zombie nor Ripcord offer technical support for these modifications. If something goes wrong, you're on your own. That said, here are some of the more interesting modifications.

DEAD BODIES MOD

ftp://ftp.f3d.net/pub/specwar/specops/mods/DeadBodiesMOD10.zip

This simple mod will increase the time it takes for enemy bodies to disappear. It works one of two ways, depending upon the mode you're in. In Sniper mode, you'll have 18 seconds to reach the body before it disappears. In Normal mode, you'll have 12 seconds to reach the corpse. This is in contrast to the standard 8 seconds in the retail version of *Spec Ops*.

RETRY MOD

ftp://ftp.f3d.net/pub/specwar/specops/mods/retryMOD.zip

Dying is no fun and you've no doubt done your fair share when playing *Spec Ops*. If you'd like to save a few keystrokes between missions, this is the mod for you. This simple mod will allow you to quickly restart the mission you were on with the same loadout as before.

RUSSIAN'S COMPASS MOD

ftp://ftp.f3d.net/pub/specwar/specops/mods/compass10.zip

This small mod permits you to see compass directions at any time while playing *Spec Ops*. Currently, when you go into ACOG or other Sniper mode, the GPS shuts down. By installing this mod, you'll be able to see the GPS reading at any time, no matter what the situation.

Future plans for this mod include adding a directional indicator to point to the next waypoint, without having you spin in a circle first.

RUSSIAN'S RANGER MOD

ftp://ftp.f3d.net/pub/specwar/specops/mods/rushianmods.zip

This mod adds a couple of handy features you might enjoy. If you ever wished your night-vision goggles would automatically reactivate after exiting Sniper mode, you want Russian's Ranger Mod. The second feature is an add-on hot key for the medkit. Instead of opening the inventory and manually selecting medkit, add this mod and press the M button to select medkit.

PATCHES

http://www.ripcordgames.com/games/specops/index.html

http://www.zombie.com

This area only applies to owners of the original *Spec Ops: Rangers Lead the Way*. If you bought the game and didn't take time to update with the latest patches, you are missing several features. These patches are available at either Zombie's or Ripcord's Web addresses.

AWAL2_3DFX.EXE

This patch adds several new features to the game, including a fully automatic M4 and, best of all, the ability to outfit your squad before you enter a mission. This is only for the 3DFX version of the game. If you're running in software mode, download the file AWAL2_software.exe.

NEWTEX.EXE

This patch is only for owners of the Voodoo2 3DFX graphics acceleration card. This is a sizable download but worth the time, as you'll benefit from a set of textures that will take full advantage of your Voodoo2 card.

SPECOPS_FINAL_PATCH.ZIP

As the name implies, this is the last official patch from Zombie for *Spec Ops*: *Rangers Lead the Way*. With this patch, you can battle more intelligent enemies and randomize enemy locations before each mission.

GLOSSARY

While not every term in the glossary appears in this book, the terms will help in multiplayer games when you need to get information to your squad as fast as possible. Simple code communicates more quickly than a long sentence. You'll save time with these codes and communicate like a real Ranger.

16 Standard military rifle

122 Enemy weapon

22 22-caliber weapon; light pistol

203 40-mm grenade launcher mounted under a rifle barrel

50 50-caliber machine gun

51 Enemy weapon: 51-caliber machine gun

AK AK47; an enemy weapon; standard Warsaw Pact rifle

Ambush Surprise attack

AO Area of operations

ARVN Army of the Republic of Vietnam

Bird Aircraft, usually a helicopter

Black Bird USAF Special Operations aircraft painted black

Bunker Protective shelter

C&C Command and control

Claymore Directional mine

Conex Large metal military container

Cover one's six Watch the rear; also "Watch your six"

CQB Close quarter battle

Didi In Vietnamese, to flee or leave rapidly

E&E Escape and evasion

Execution Steps required to complete a mission

Exfil Exfiltration; to leave; point of exit from AO

Fire fan Field of fire of larger gun or mortar

First shirt First Sergeant, usually highest enlisted grade in company

Flak vest Increases armor

Grease To kill

HQ Headquarters

IA Immediate action

Infiltrate Enter area covertly

Insert Insertion; point of entrance into AO

Intel Intelligence information

KIA Killed in action

LZ Landing zone, a site for helicopter to land

LZ watcher Enemy guard who reports activity in LZ

Medivac Medical evacuation of injured personnel

MIA Missing in action

NLT Not later than

NVA North Vietnamese Army

OP Observation post

OP ORD Operation orders

PH Purple Heart awarded for wounds received in action

Point or point man First soldier in formation; the scout

POW Prisoner of war

Reckless Slang, a recoilless rifle, small artillery piece

RON Remain over night, a nighttime position

RPD Enemy weapon, light squad machine gun

RT Recon team

SATCOM Satellite communications

SF Special forces

SOG Special operations group

Stabo rig Web gear that aids in lifting wearer into harness

Straphang Operate with a team other than one's own

Tail Soldier who walks last in formation, covers the rear

TOC Tactical operations center

Tracer Military round that leaves a visible trail as it travels

Ville Village

Watcher See LZ watcher

WP Short for willie pete, which is white phosphorus round or grenade